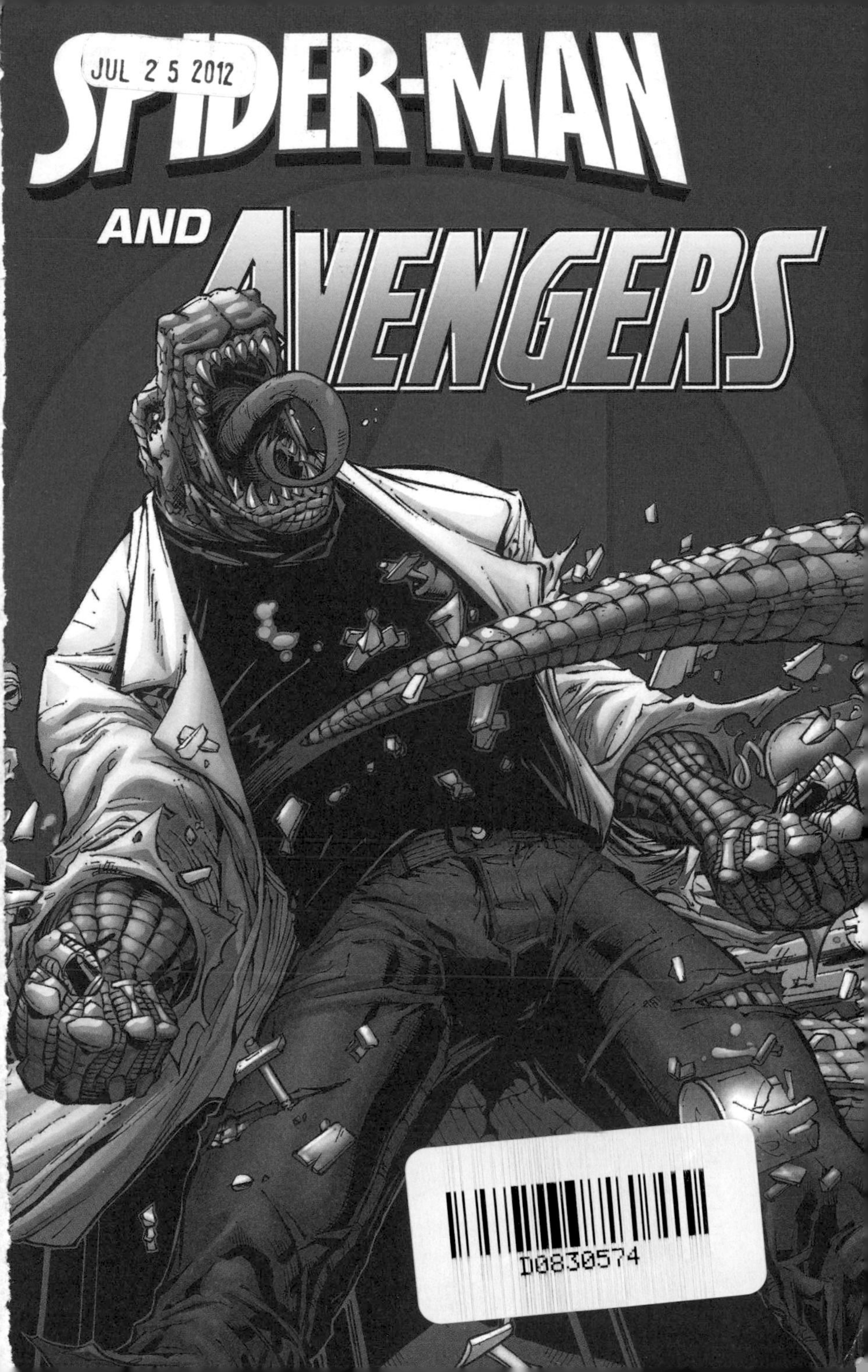
SPIDER-MAN
AND AVENGERS

SPIDER-MAN
AND THE AVENGERS

"Face to Face with the Lizard!"
Plot: **Stan Lee & Steve Ditko**
Script: **Daniel Quantz**
Penciler: **Jonboy Meyers**
Inker: **Pat Davidson**
Colorist: **Udon's Larry Molinar**
Udon Chief: **Erik Ko**
Letterer: **VC's Randy Gentile**
Cover Artists: **Mark Brooks & Udon**
Assistant Editors: **Mackenzie Cadenhead & Nick Lowe**
Editor: **C.B. Cebulski**
Consulting Editor: **Ralph Macchio**

"Loki Laughs Last"
Writer: **Tony Bedard**
Penciler: **Shannon Gallant**
Inker: **Norman Lee**
Colorist: **Impacto Studios' Adriano Lucas**
Letterer: **Dave Sharpe**
Cover Artists: **Sean Chen, Sandu Florea & Guru e-FX**
Assistant Editor: **Nathan Cosby**
Editor: **Mark Paniccia**

"I, Reptile!"
Writer: **Zeb Wells**
Penciler: **Patrick Scherberger**
Inker: **Norman Lee**
Colorist: **Guru e-FX**
Cover Artists: **Amanda Connor & Christina Strain**
Letterer: **Dave Sharpe**
Assistant Editor: **Nathan Cosby**
Editors: **Mackenzie Cadenhead with Mark Paniccia**

"Bringers of the Storm"
Writer: **Jeff Parker**
Penciler: **Cafu**
Inker: **Terry Pallot**
Colorist: **Val Staples**
Letterer: **Dave Sharpe**
Cover Artists: **Leonard Kirk, Terry Pallot
& Chris Sotomayor**
Assistant Editor: **Nathan Cosby**
Editor: **Mark Paniccia**

Collection Editor: **Cory Levine**
Assistant Editors: **Alex Starbuck & Nelson Ribeiro**
Editors, Special Projects: **Jennifer Grünwald & Mark D. Beazley**
Senior Editor, Special Projects: **Jeff Youngquist**
Senior Vice President of Sales: **David Gabriel**
SVP of Brand Planning & Communications: **Michael Pasciullo**

Editor in Chief: **Axel Alonso**
Chief Creative Officer: **Joe Quesada**
Publisher: **Dan Buckley**
Executive Producer: **Alan Fine**

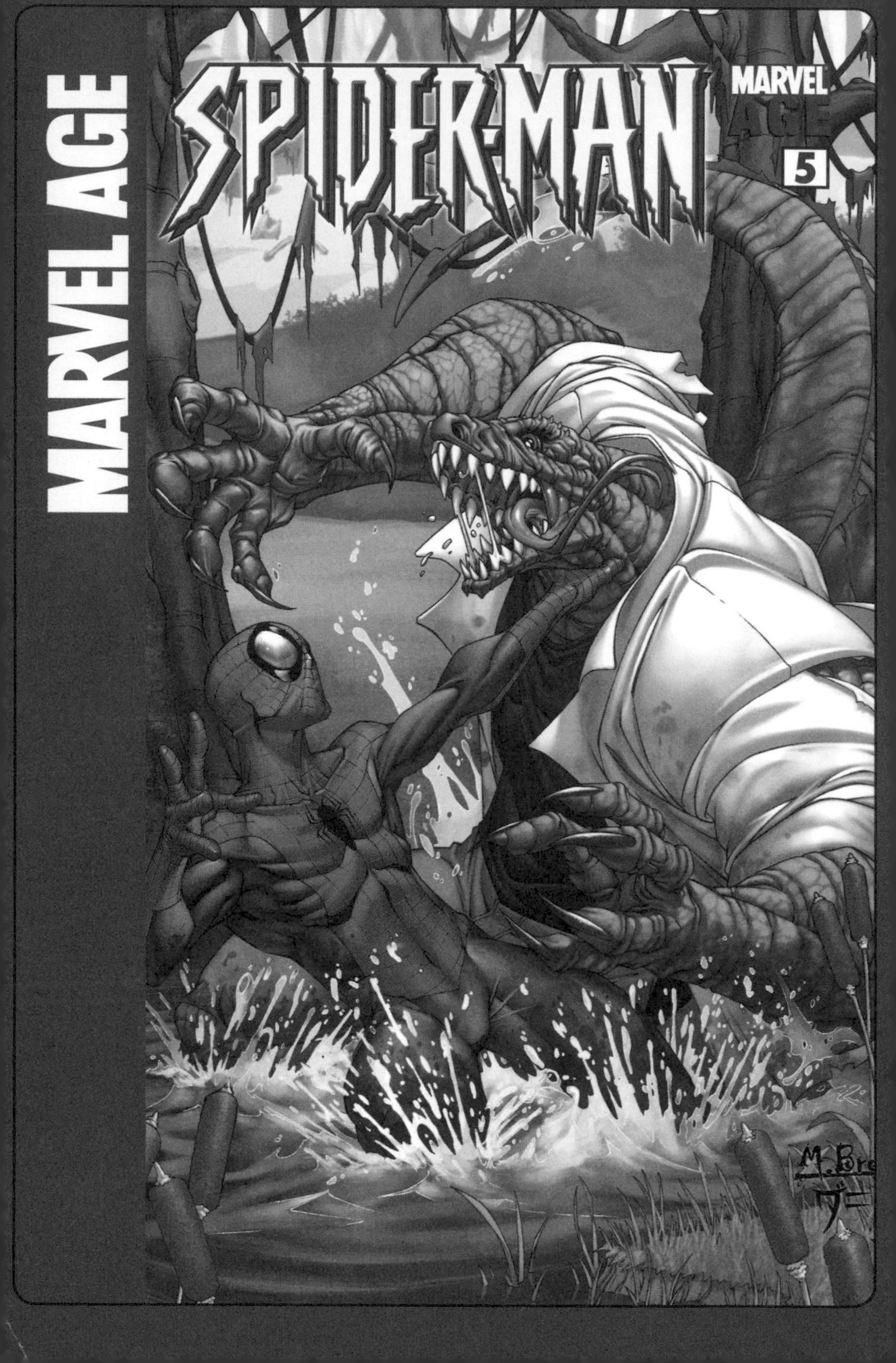
MARVEL AGE
SPIDER-MAN
MARVEL AGE
5

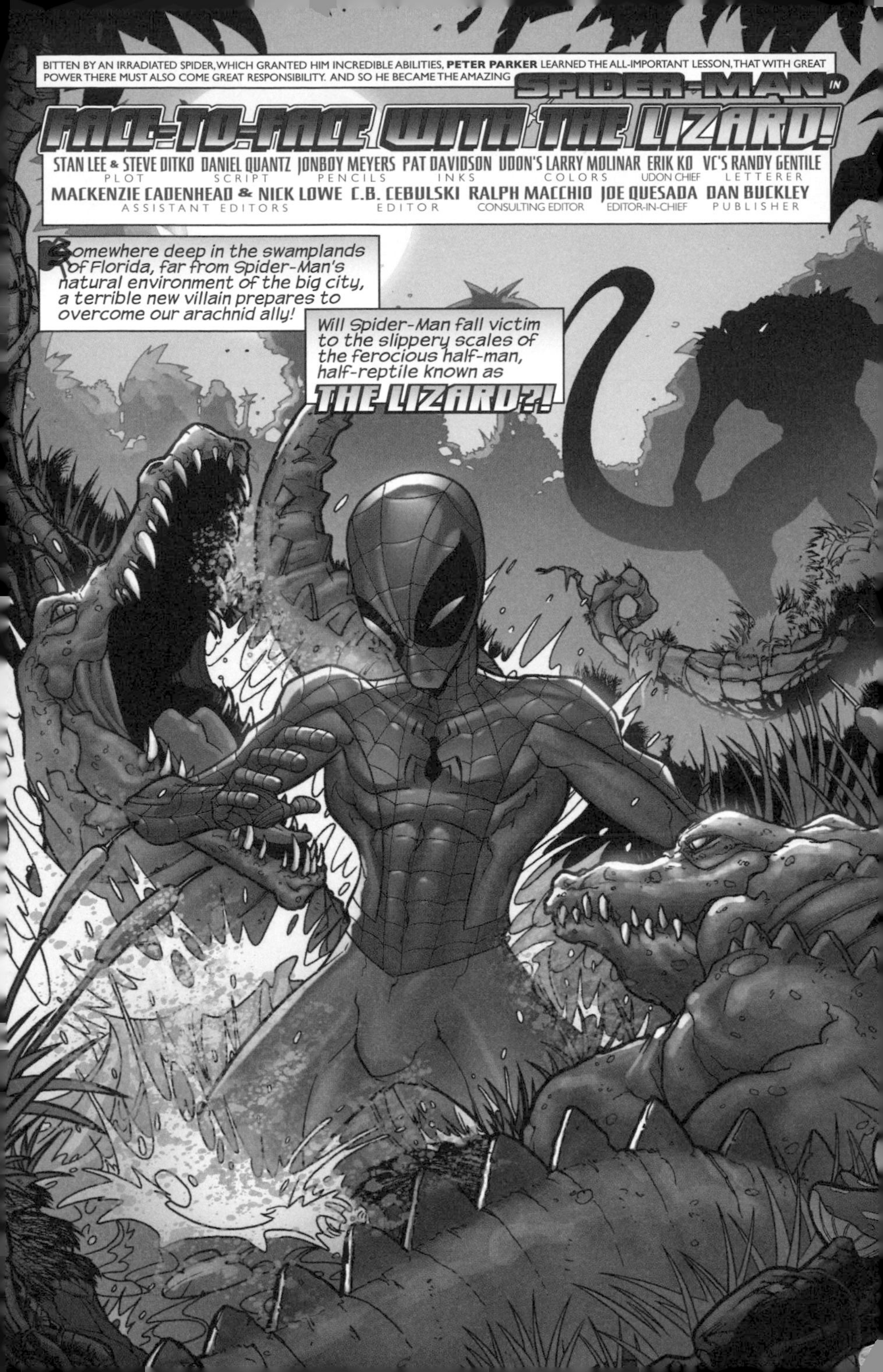
BITTEN BY AN IRRADIATED SPIDER, WHICH GRANTED HIM INCREDIBLE ABILITIES, PETER PARKER LEARNED THE ALL-IMPORTANT LESSON, THAT WITH GREAT POWER THERE MUST ALSO COME GREAT RESPONSIBILITY. AND SO HE BECAME THE AMAZING SPIDER-MAN IN
FACE-TO-FACE WITH THE LIZARD!
STAN LEE & STEVE DITKO PLOT DANIEL QUANTZ SCRIPT JONBOY MEYERS PENCILS PAT DAVIDSON INKS UDON'S LARRY MOLINAR COLORS ERIK KO UDON CHIEF VC'S RANDY GENTILE LETTERER
MACKENZIE CADENHEAD & NICK LOWE ASSISTANT EDITORS C.B. CEBULSKI EDITOR RALPH MACCHIO CONSULTING EDITOR JOE QUESADA EDITOR-IN-CHIEF DAN BUCKLEY PUBLISHER
Somewhere deep in the swamplands of Florida, far from Spider-Man's natural environment of the big city, a terrible new villain prepares to overcome our arachnid ally!
Will Spider-Man fall victim to the slippery scales of the ferocious half-man, half-reptile known as THE LIZARD?!

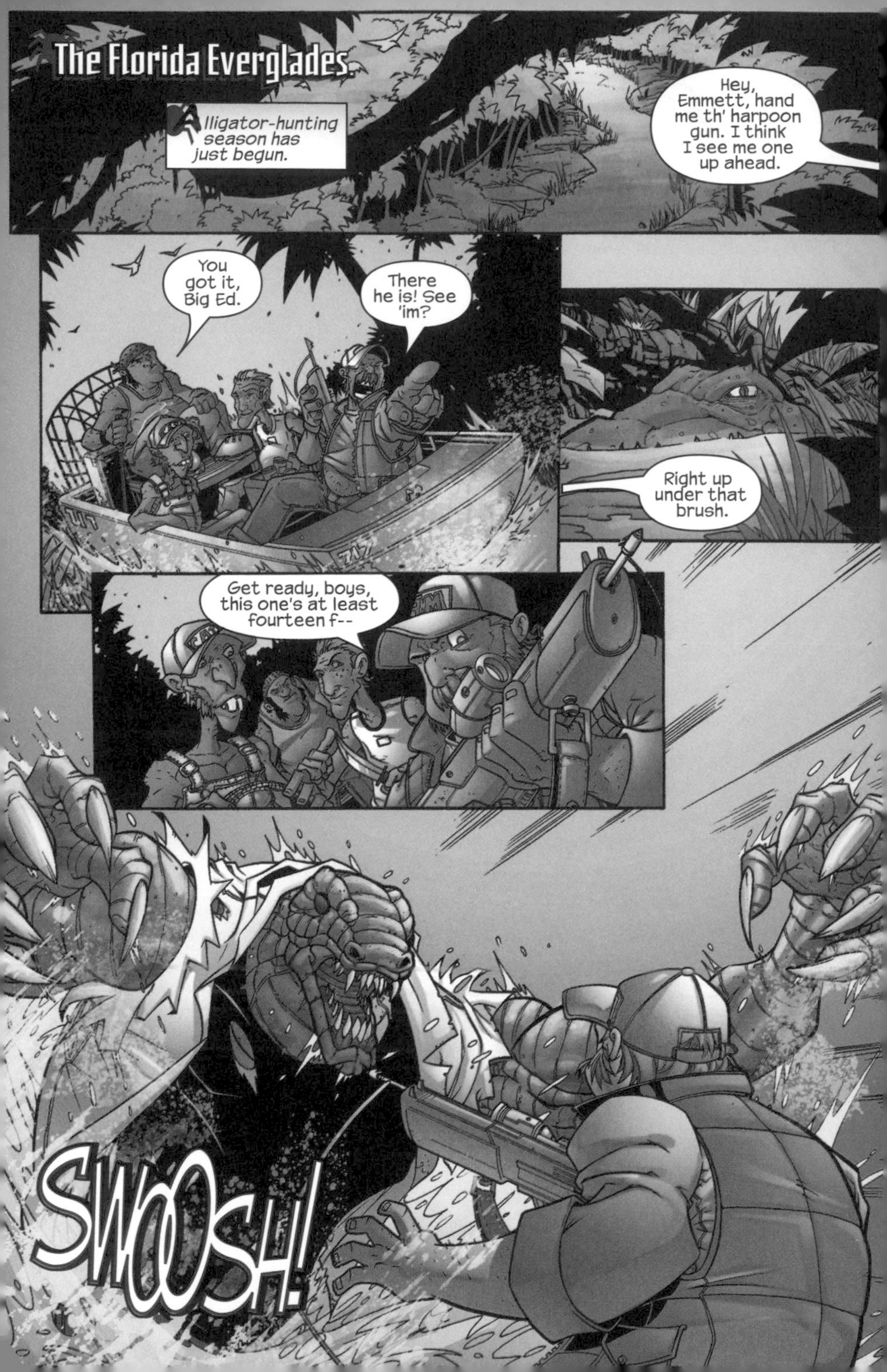
The Florida Everglades.
Alligator-hunting season has just begun.
Hey, Emmett, hand me th' harpoon gun. I think I see me one up ahead.
You got it, Big Ed.
There he is! See 'im?
Right up under that brush.
Get ready, boys, this one's at least fourteen f--
SWOOSH!

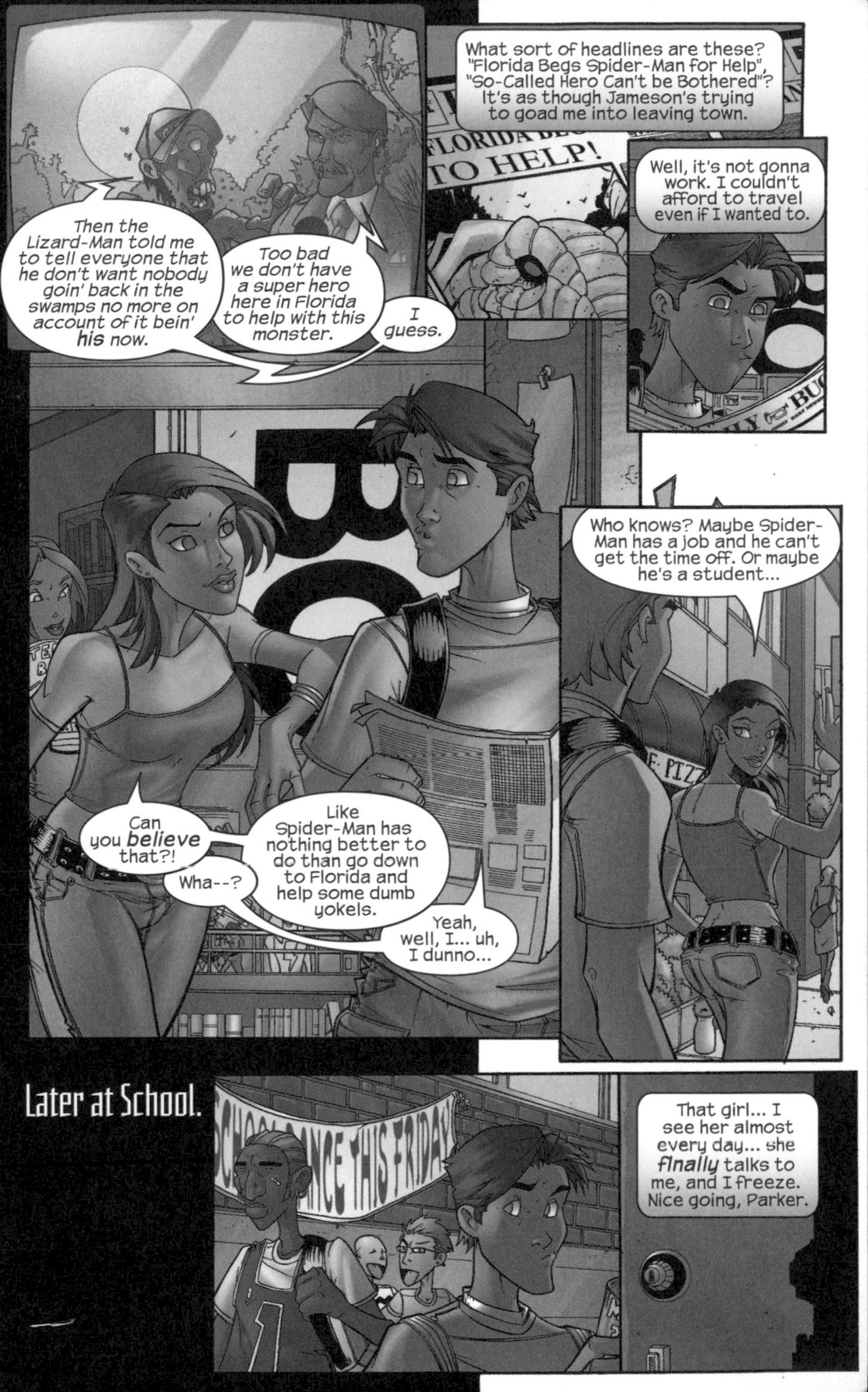
Then the Lizard-Man told me to tell everyone that he don't want nobody goin' back in the swamps no more on account of it bein' **his** now.
Too bad we don't have a super hero here in Florida to help with this monster.
I guess.
What sort of headlines are these? "Florida Begs Spider-Man for Help", "So-Called Hero Can't be Bothered"? It's as though Jameson's trying to goad me into leaving town.
TO HELP!
Well, it's not gonna work. I couldn't afford to travel even if I wanted to.
Can you *believe* that?!
Like Spider-Man has nothing better to do than go down to Florida and help some dumb yokels.
Wha--?
Yeah, well, I... uh, I dunno...
Who knows? Maybe Spider-Man has a job and he can't get the time off. Or maybe he's a student...
Later at School.
That girl... I see her almost every day... she *finally* talks to me, and I freeze. Nice going, Parker.

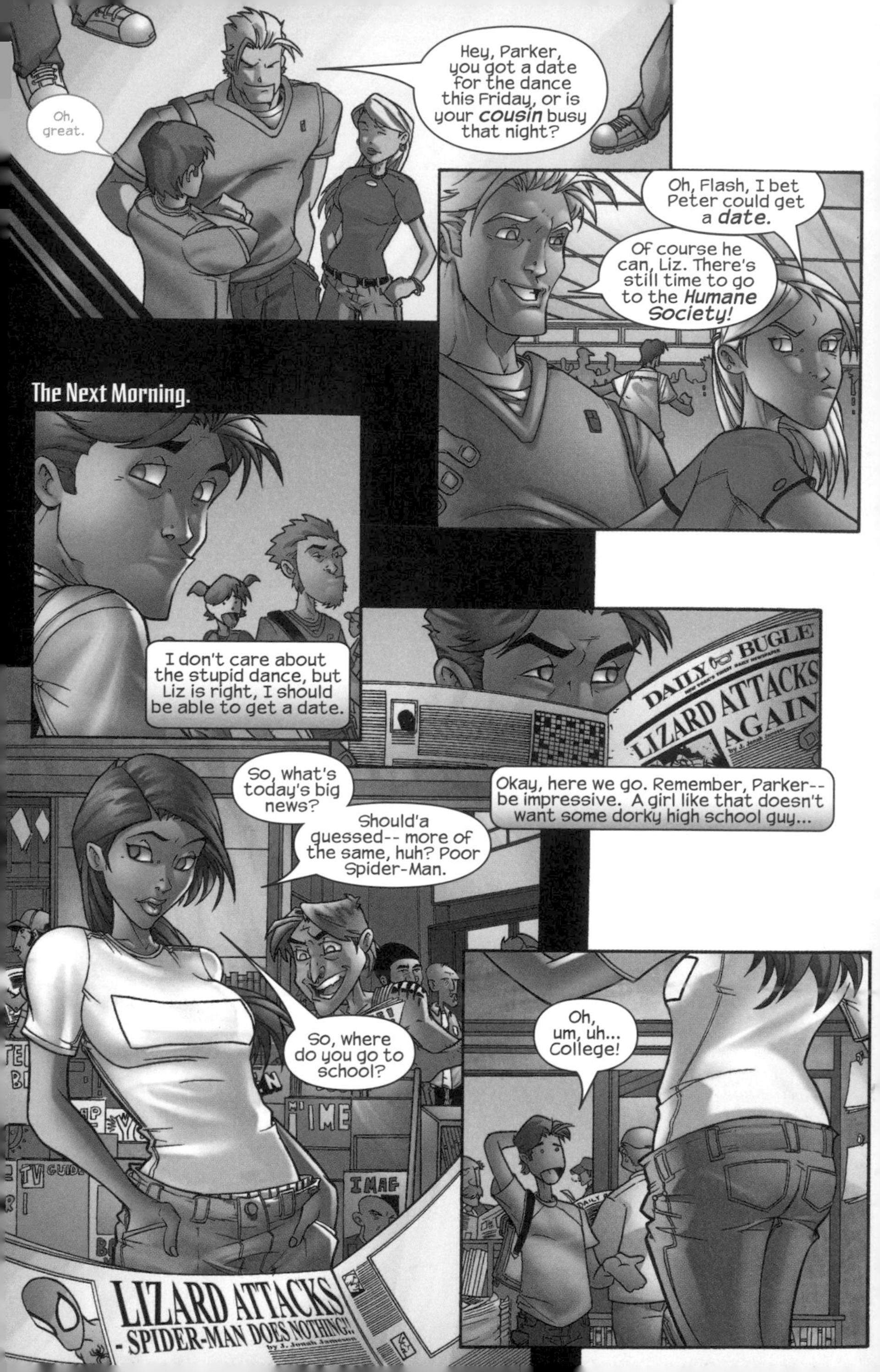
Hey, Parker, you got a date for the dance this Friday, or is your *cousin* busy that night?
Oh, great.
Oh, Flash, I bet Peter could get a *date.*
Of course he can, Liz. There's still time to go to the *Humane Society!*
The Next Morning.
I don't care about the stupid dance, but Liz is right, I should be able to get a date.
DAILY BUGLE
LIZARD ATTACKS AGAIN
Okay, here we go. Remember, Parker-- be impressive. A girl like that doesn't want some dorky high school guy...
So, what's today's big news?
Should'a guessed-- more of the same, huh? Poor Spider-Man.
So, where do you go to school?
Oh, um, uh... College!
LIZARD ATTACKS
- SPIDER-MAN DOES NOTHING!!
by J. Jonah Jameson

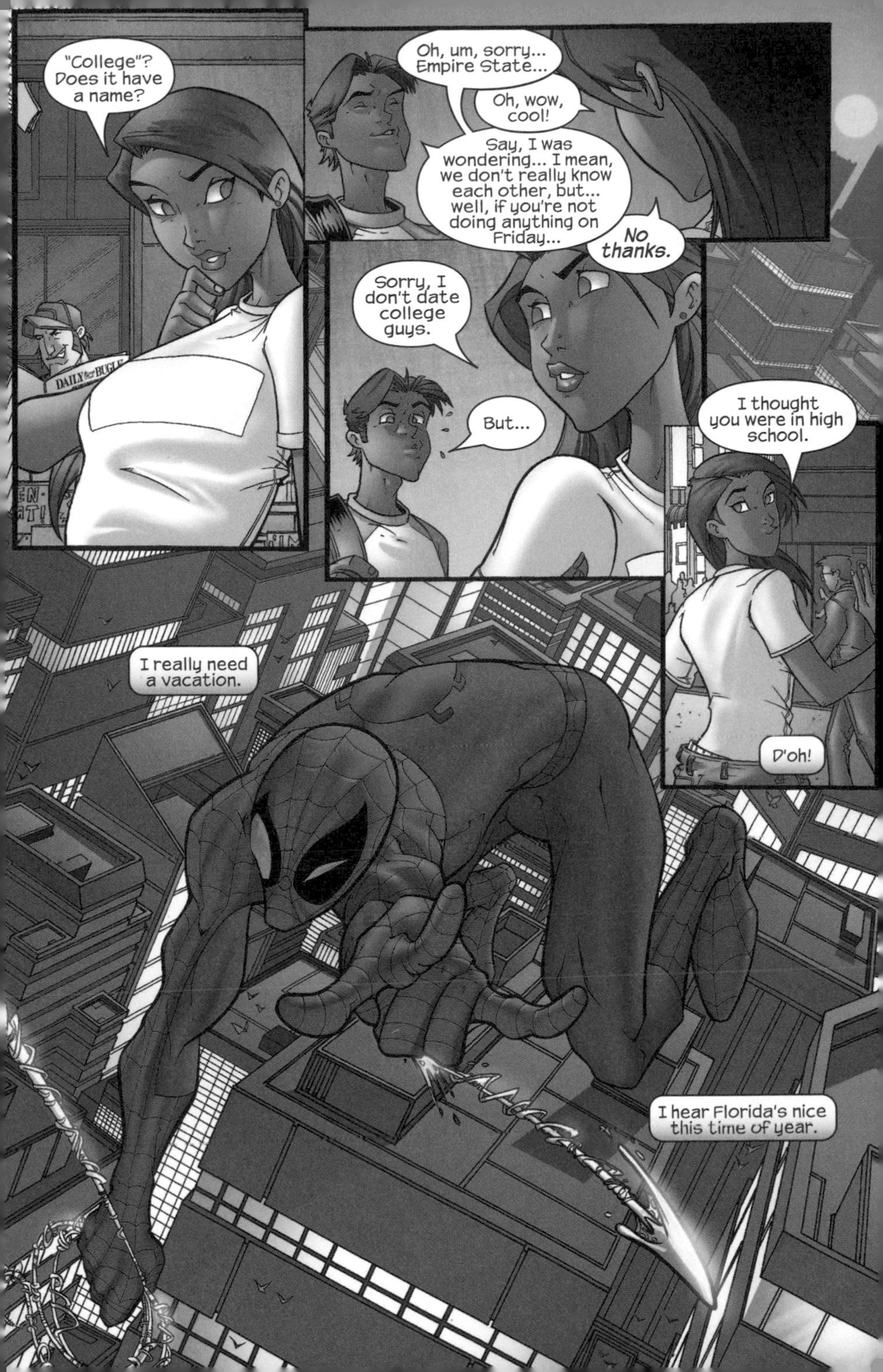
"College"? Does it have a name?
Oh, um, sorry... Empire State...
Oh, wow, cool!
Say, I was wondering... I mean, we don't really know each other, but... well, if you're not doing anything on Friday...
No thanks.
Sorry, I don't date college guys.
But...
I thought you were in high school.
D'oh!
I really need a vacation.
I hear Florida's nice this time of year.

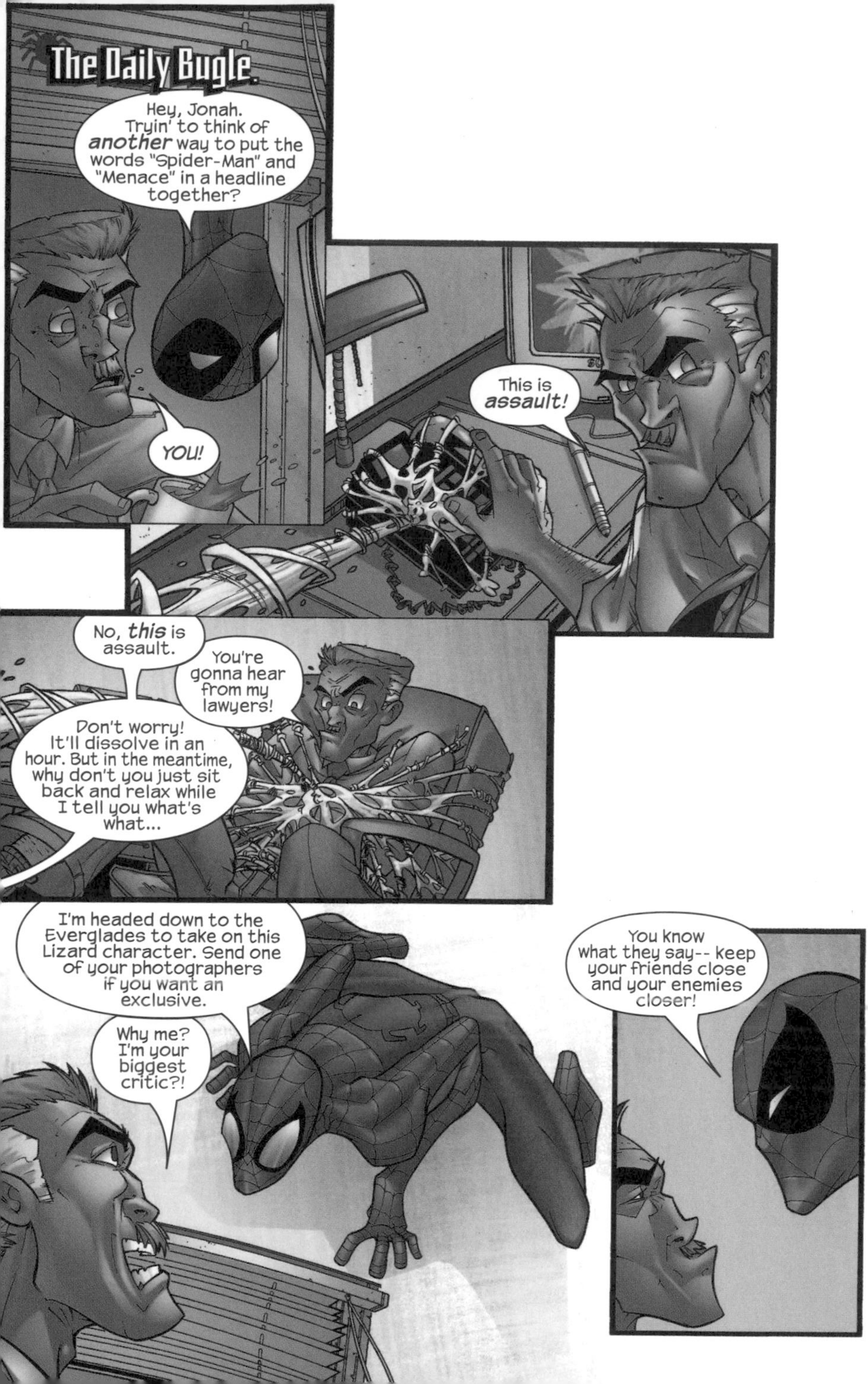

The Daily Bugle.
Hey, Jonah. Tryin' to think of *another* way to put the words "Spider-Man" and "Menace" in a headline together?
YOU!
This is *assault!*
No, *this* is assault.
You're gonna hear from my lawyers!
Don't worry! It'll dissolve in an hour. But in the meantime, why don't you just sit back and relax while I tell you what's what...
I'm headed down to the Everglades to take on this Lizard character. Send one of your photographers if you want an exclusive.
Why me? I'm your biggest critic?!
You know what they say-- keep your friends close and your enemies closer!

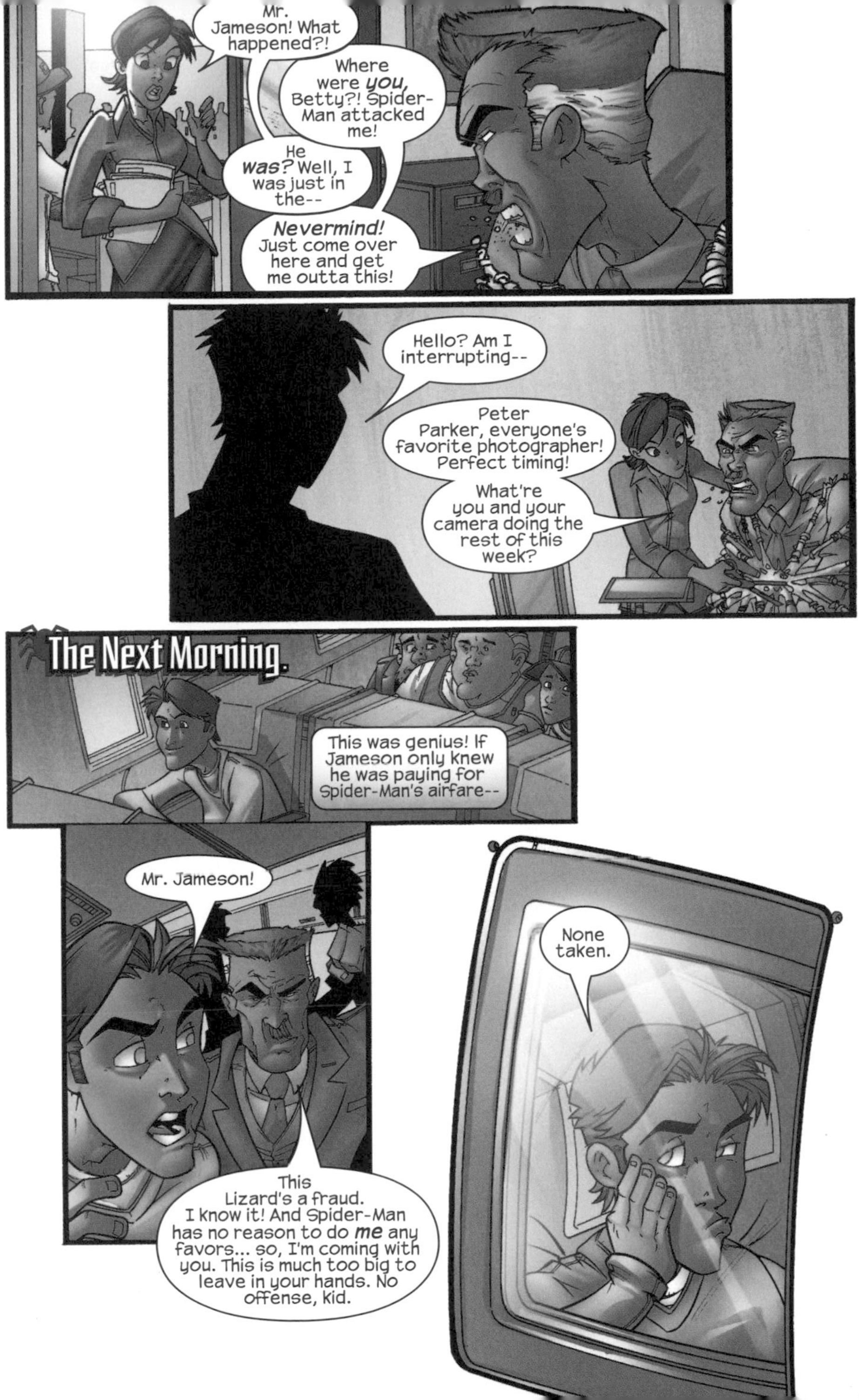
Mr. Jameson! What happened?!
Where were *you*, Betty?! Spider-Man attacked me!
He *was?* Well, I was just in the--
Nevermind! Just come over here and get me outta this!
Hello? Am I interrupting--
Peter Parker, everyone's favorite photographer! Perfect timing!
What're you and your camera doing the rest of this week?
The Next Morning.
This was genius! If Jameson only knew he was paying for Spider-Man's airfare--
Mr. Jameson!
This Lizard's a fraud. I know it! And Spider-Man has no reason to do *me* any favors... so, I'm coming with you. This is much too big to leave in your hands. No offense, kid.
None taken.

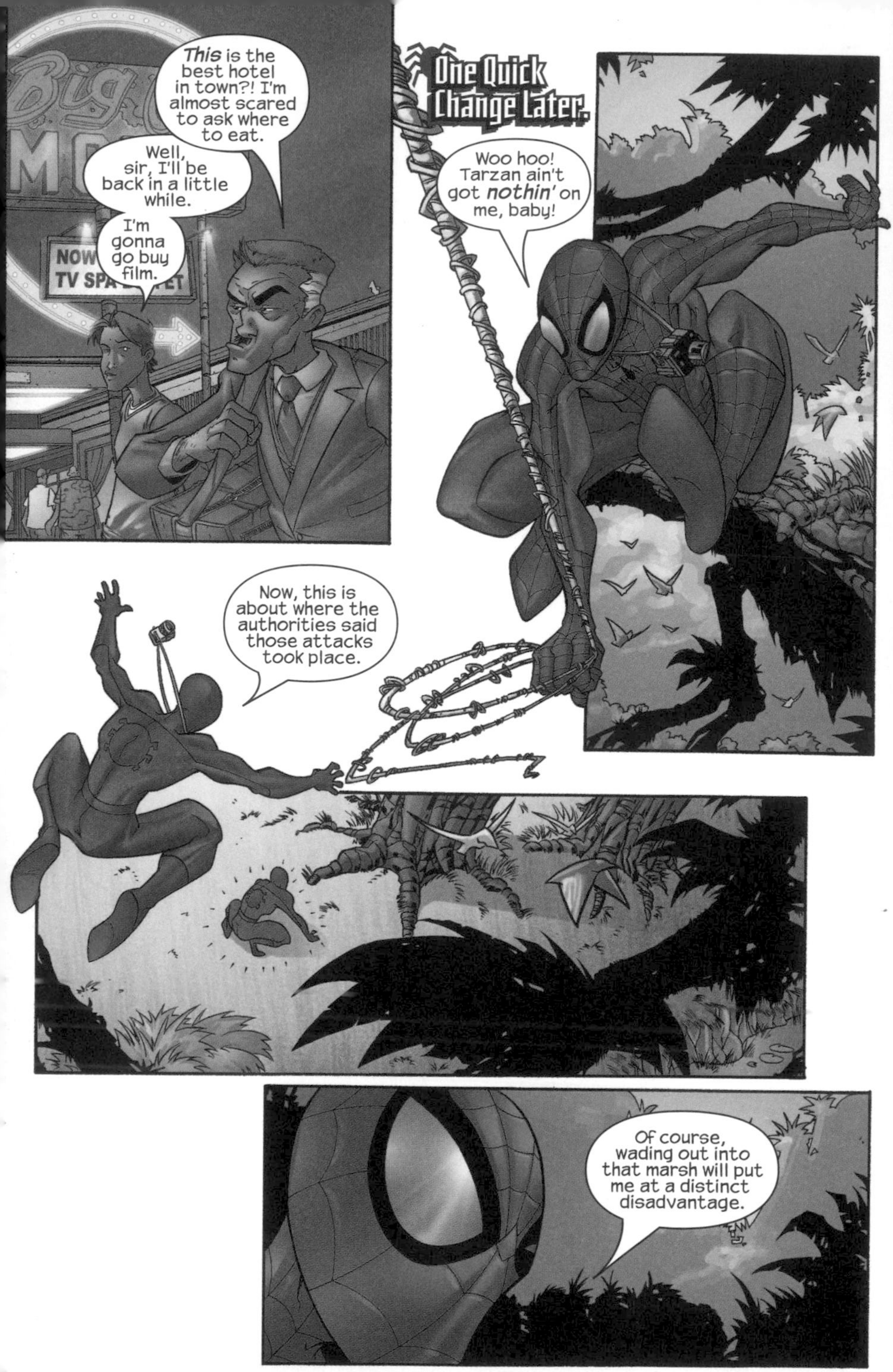
This is the best hotel in town?! I'm almost scared to ask where to eat.
Well, sir, I'll be back in a little while.
I'm gonna go buy film.
NOW
TV SPA
One Quick Change Later.
Woo hoo! Tarzan ain't got nothin' on me, baby!
Now, this is about where the authorities said those attacks took place.
Of course, wading out into that marsh will put me at a distinct disadvantage.

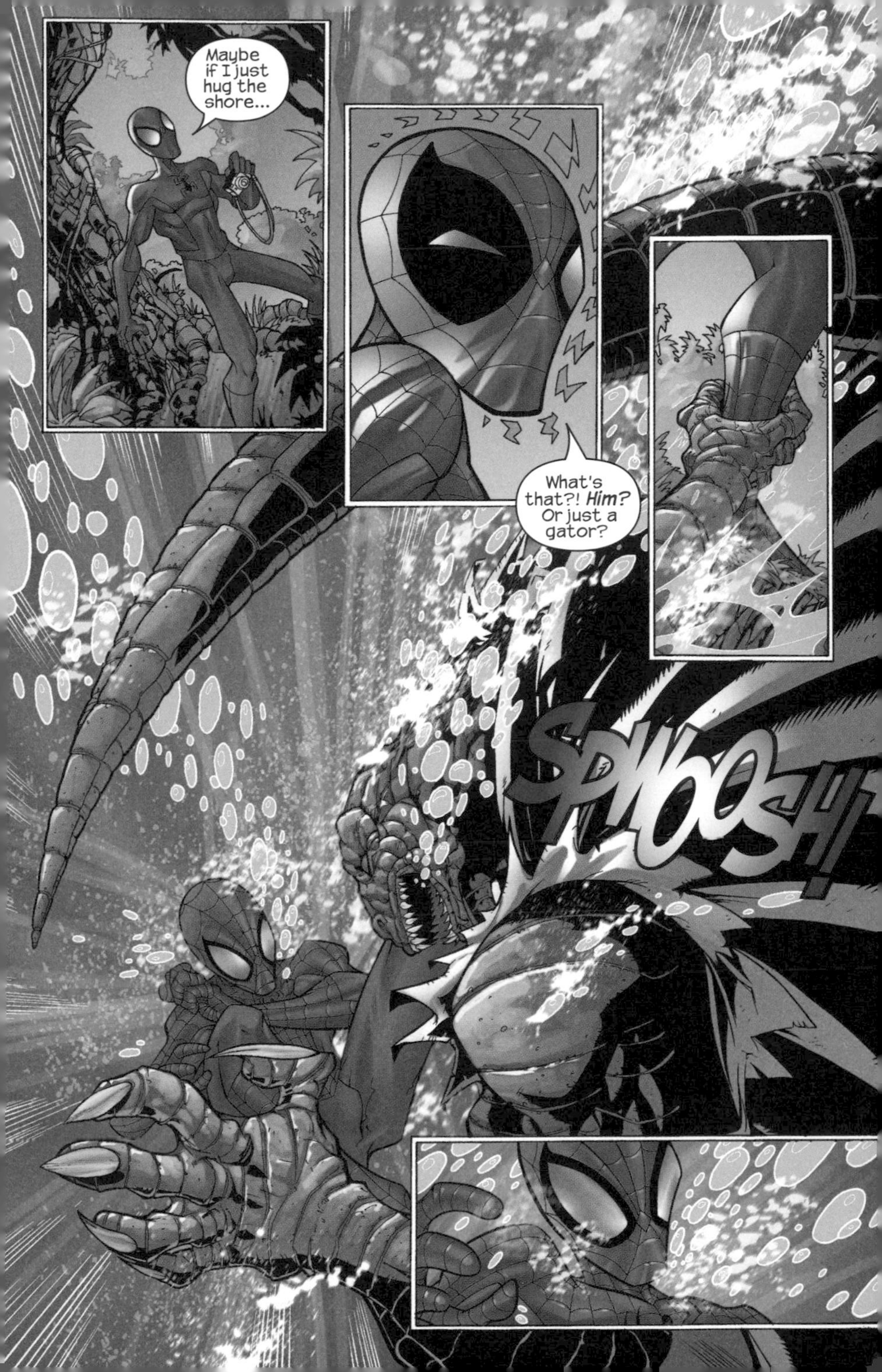
Maybe if I just hug the shore...
What's that?! *Him?* Or just a gator?
SPLOOSH!

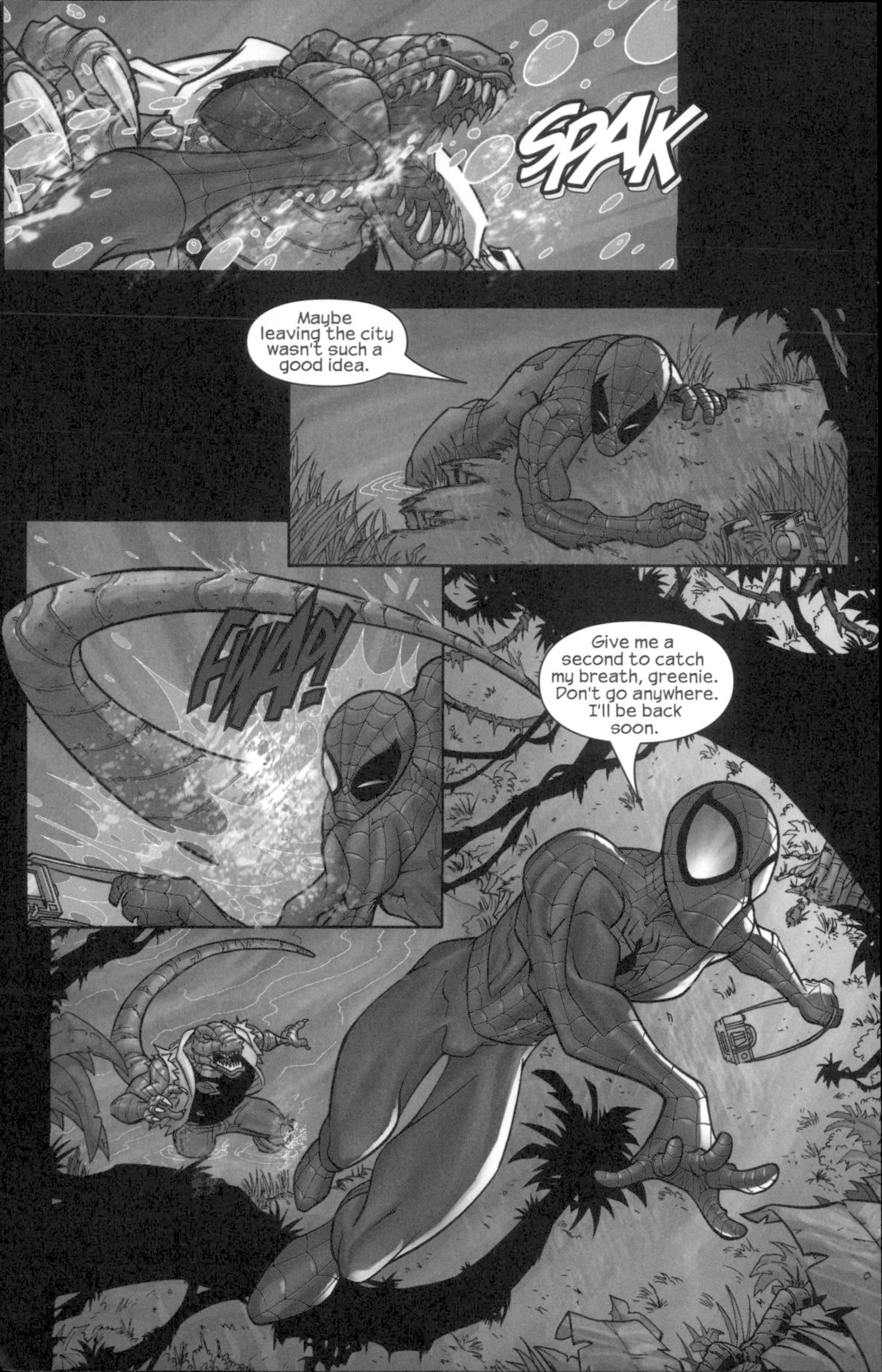
SPAK
Maybe leaving the city wasn't such a good idea.
FWAP!
Give me a second to catch my breath, greenie. Don't go anywhere. I'll be back soon.

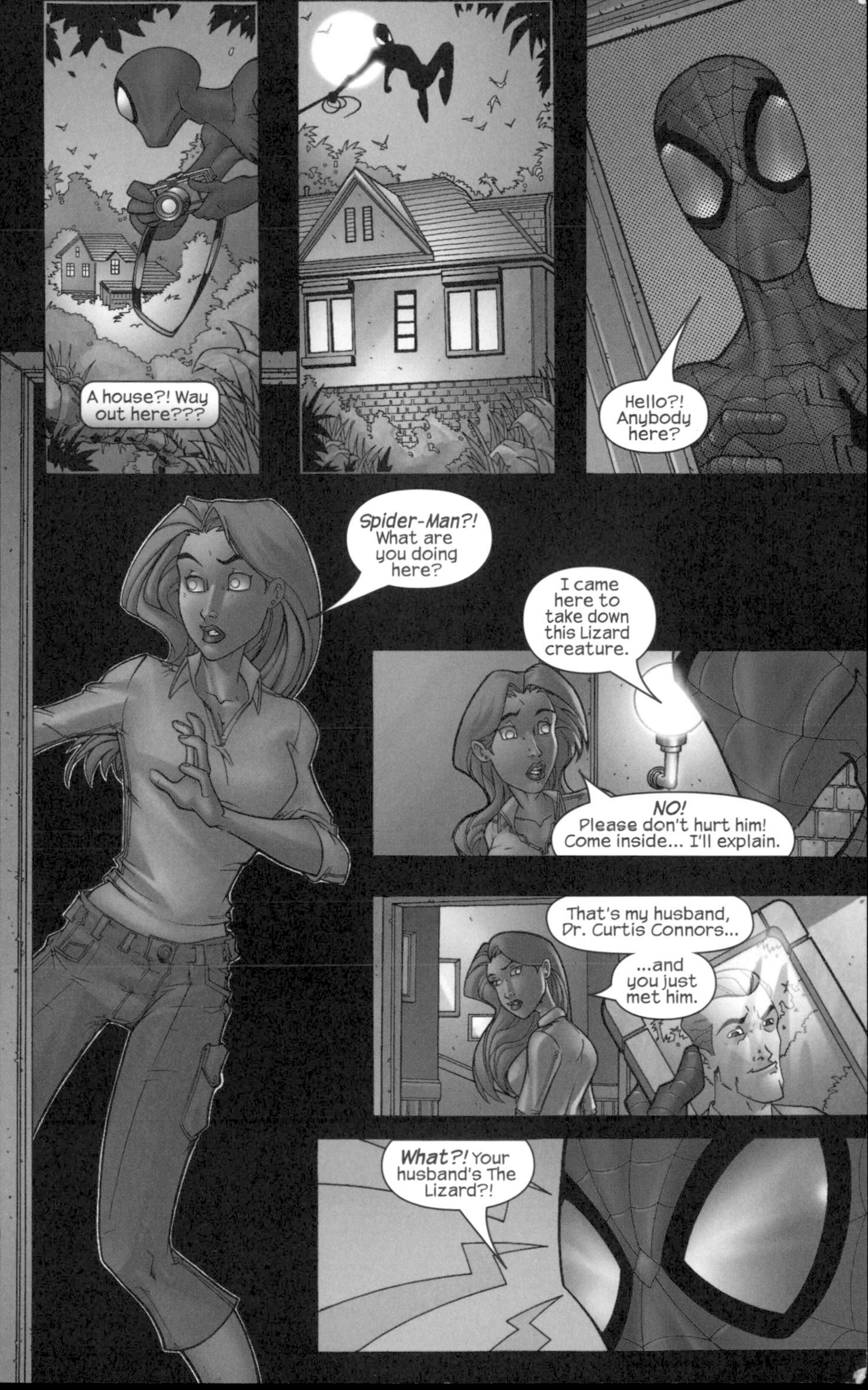
A house?! Way out here???
Hello?! Anybody here?
Spider-Man?! What are you doing here?
I came here to take down this Lizard creature.
NO! Please don't hurt him! Come inside... I'll explain.
That's my husband, Dr. Curtis Connors...
...and you just met him.
What?! Your husband's The Lizard?!

"We met in college. He was so handsome, studying to be a physician.

"He was in the Army Reserves and was sent to Kosovo. We thought everything would be okay.

"So, he developed a serum that could give other animals the same ability, testing it first on rabbits... it was miraculous!

"The truth is, I never could get used to the missing arm, and he knew it. So it was inevitable that one day...

"He would try to become whole again.

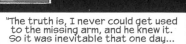

"I wish I could say I was happy when it worked, but deep down I knew...

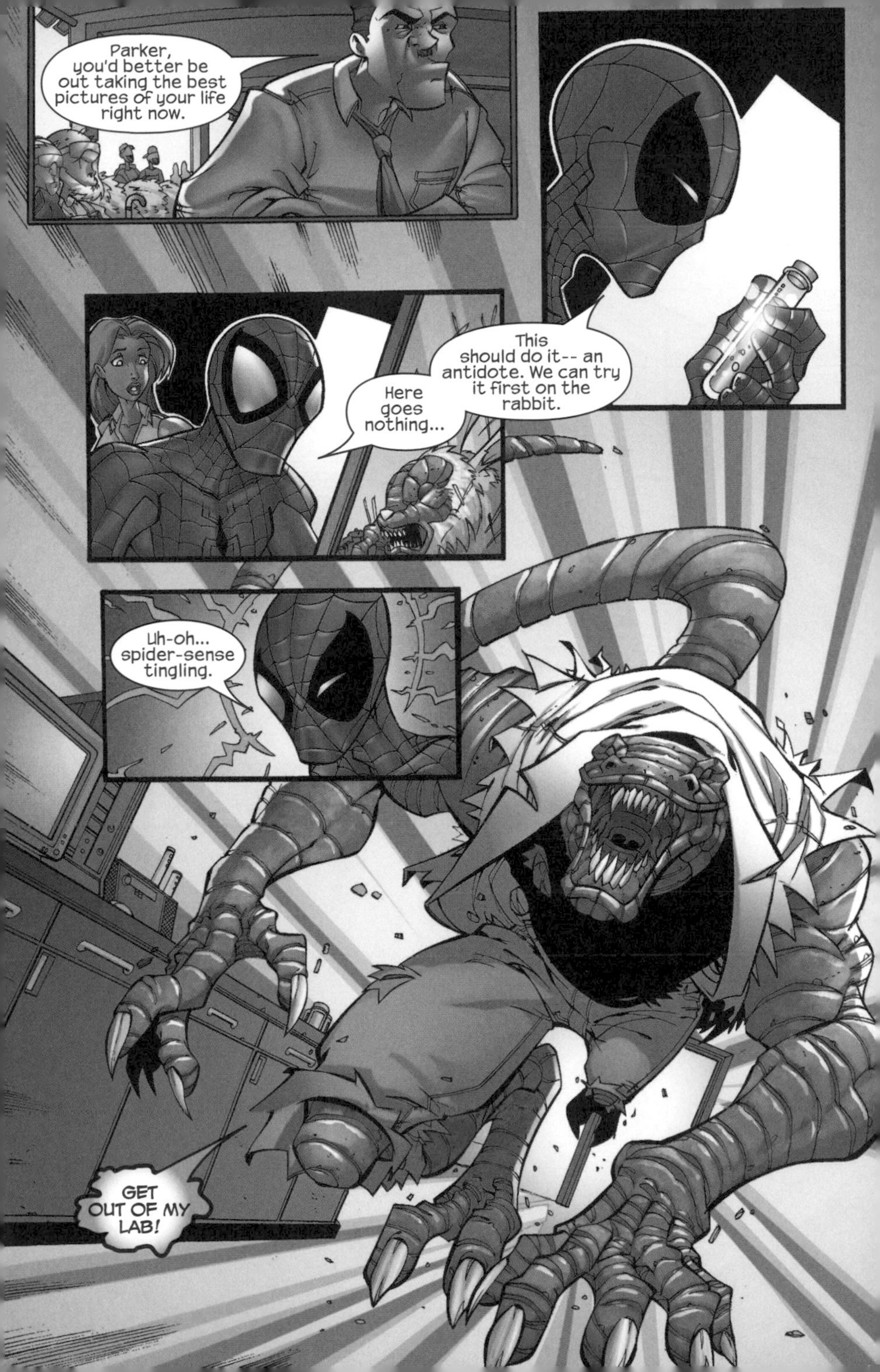
Parker, you'd better be out taking the best pictures of your life right now.
This should do it-- an antidote. We can try it first on the rabbit.
Here goes nothing...
Uh-oh... spider-sense tingling.
GET OUT OF MY LAB!

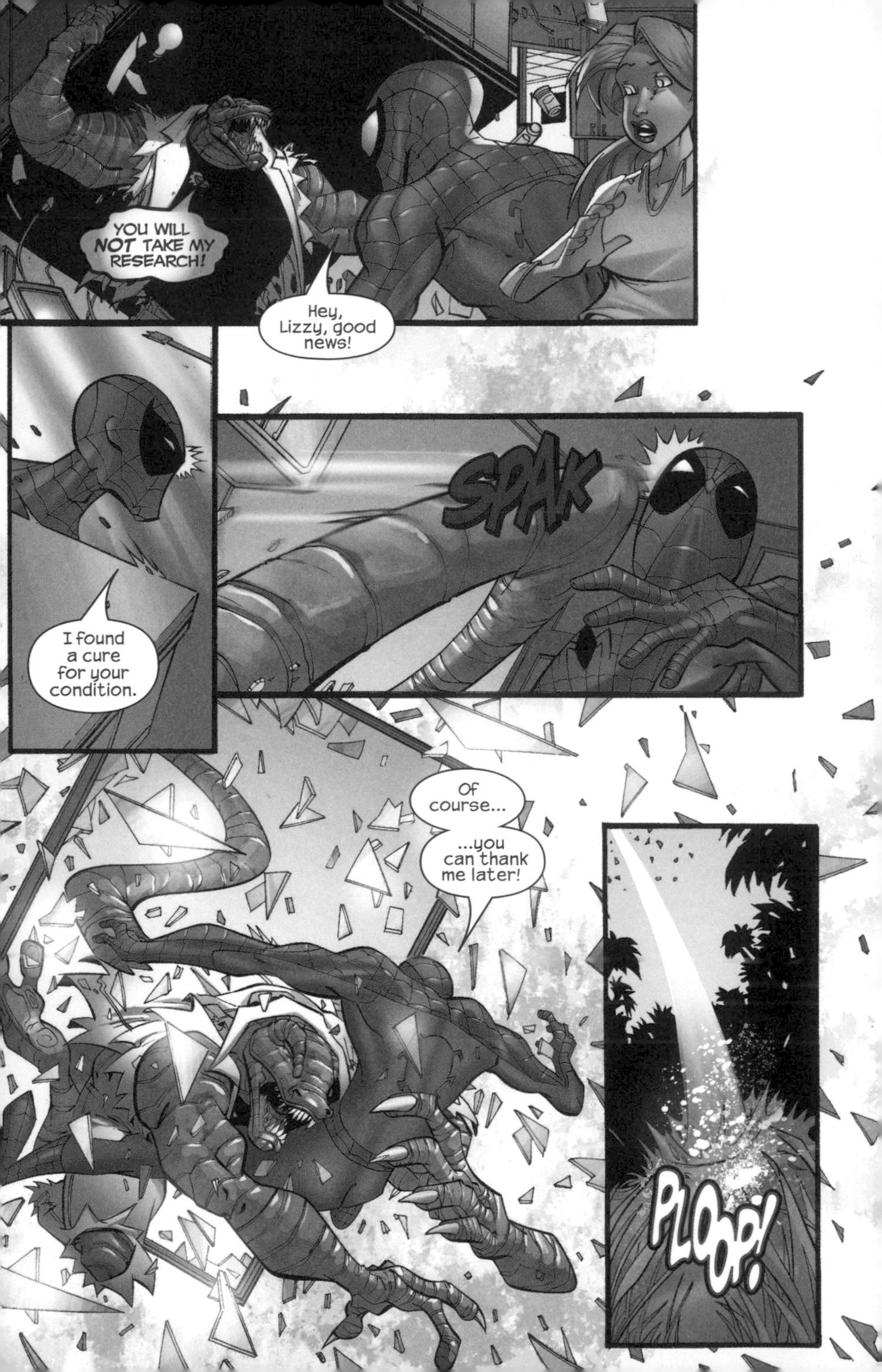
YOU WILL NOT TAKE MY RESEARCH!
Hey, Lizzy, good news!
I found a cure for your condition.
SPAK
Of course...
...you can thank me later!
PLOOP!

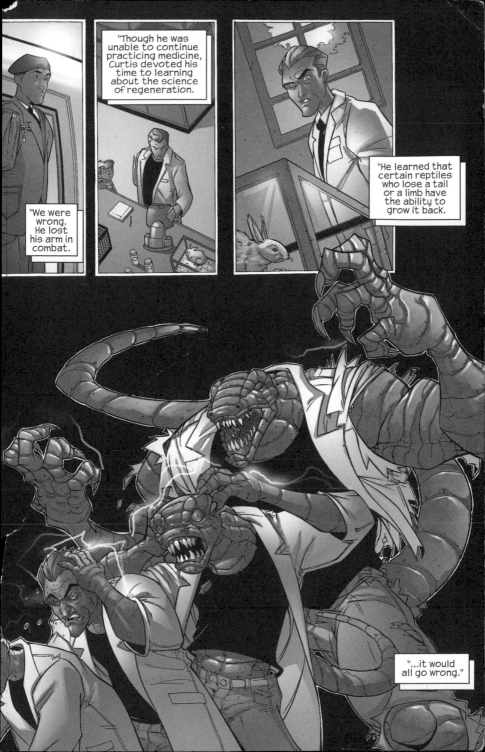

"Though he was unable to continue practicing medicine, Curtis devoted his time to learning about the science of regeneration.

"We were wrong. He lost his arm in combat.

"He learned that certain reptiles who lose a tail or a limb have the ability to grow it back.

"...it would all go wrong."

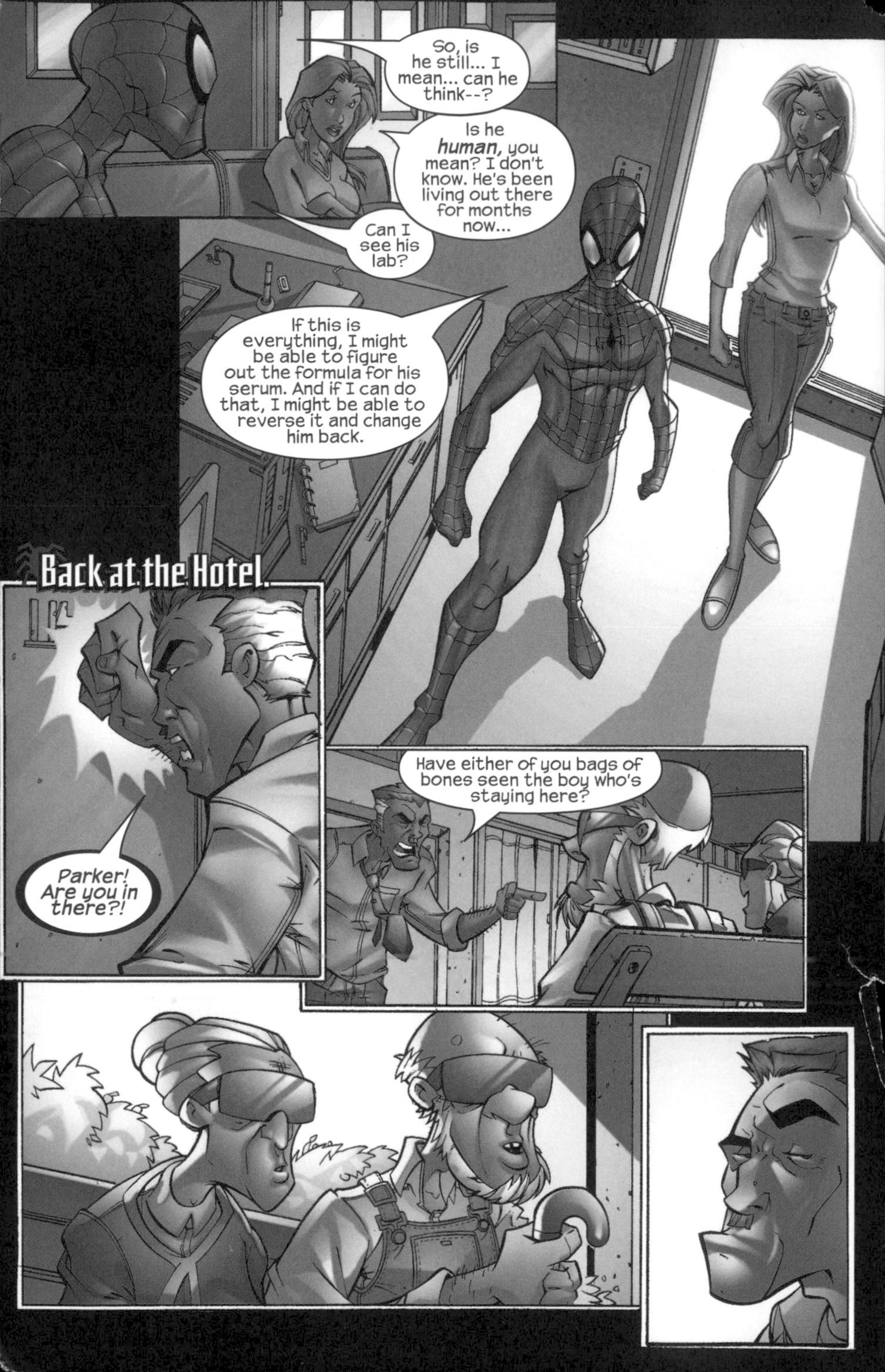
So, is he still... I mean... can he think--?
Is he *human,* you mean? I don't know. He's been living out there for months now...
Can I see his lab?
If this is everything, I might be able to figure out the formula for his serum. And if I can do that, I might be able to reverse it and change him back.
Back at the Hotel.
Parker! Are you in there?!
Have either of you bags of bones seen the boy who's staying here?

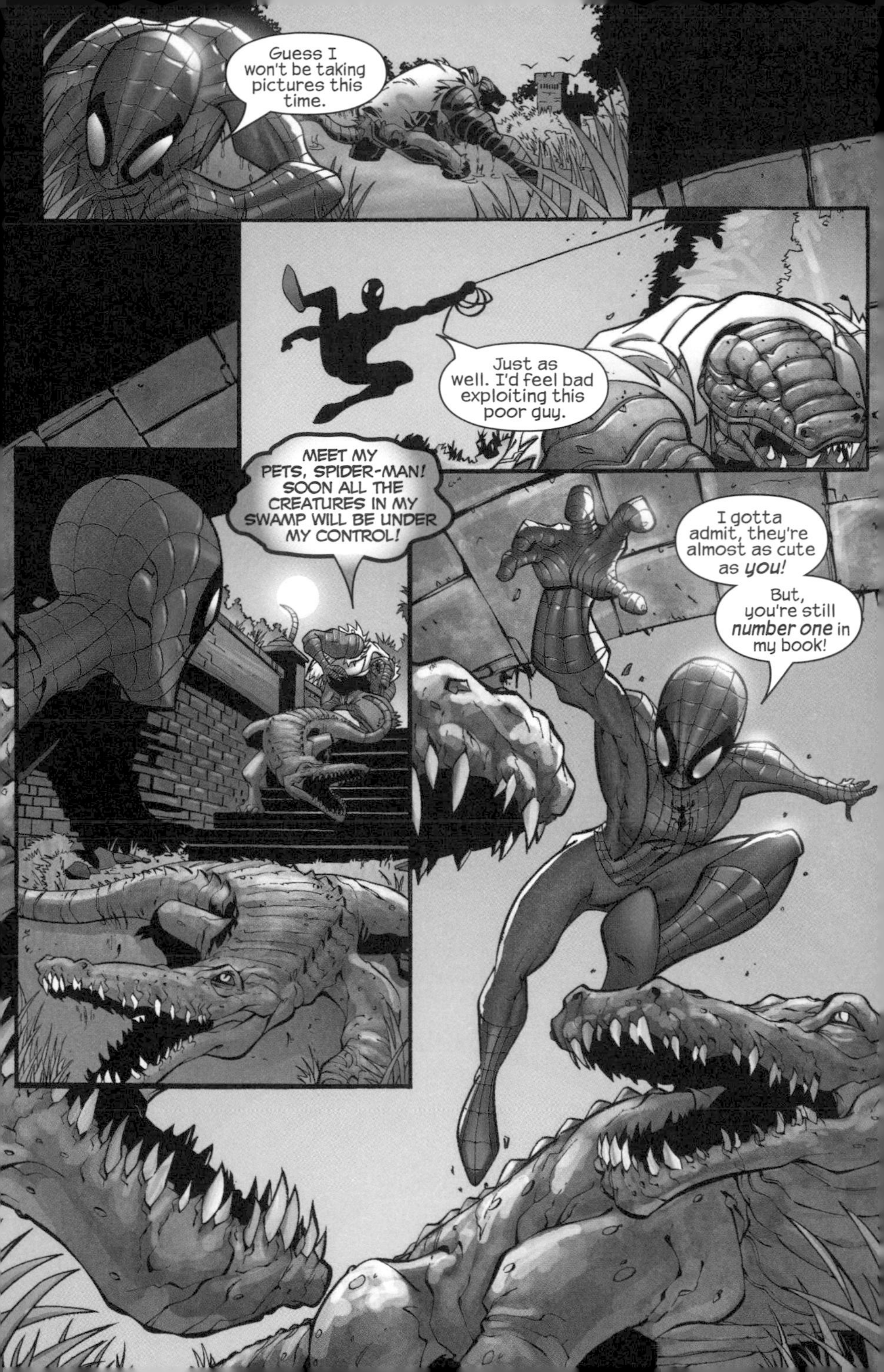
Guess I won't be taking pictures this time.
Just as well. I'd feel bad exploiting this poor guy.
MEET MY PETS, SPIDER-MAN! SOON ALL THE CREATURES IN MY SWAMP WILL BE UNDER MY CONTROL!
I gotta admit, they're almost as cute as *you!*
But, you're still ***number one*** in my book!

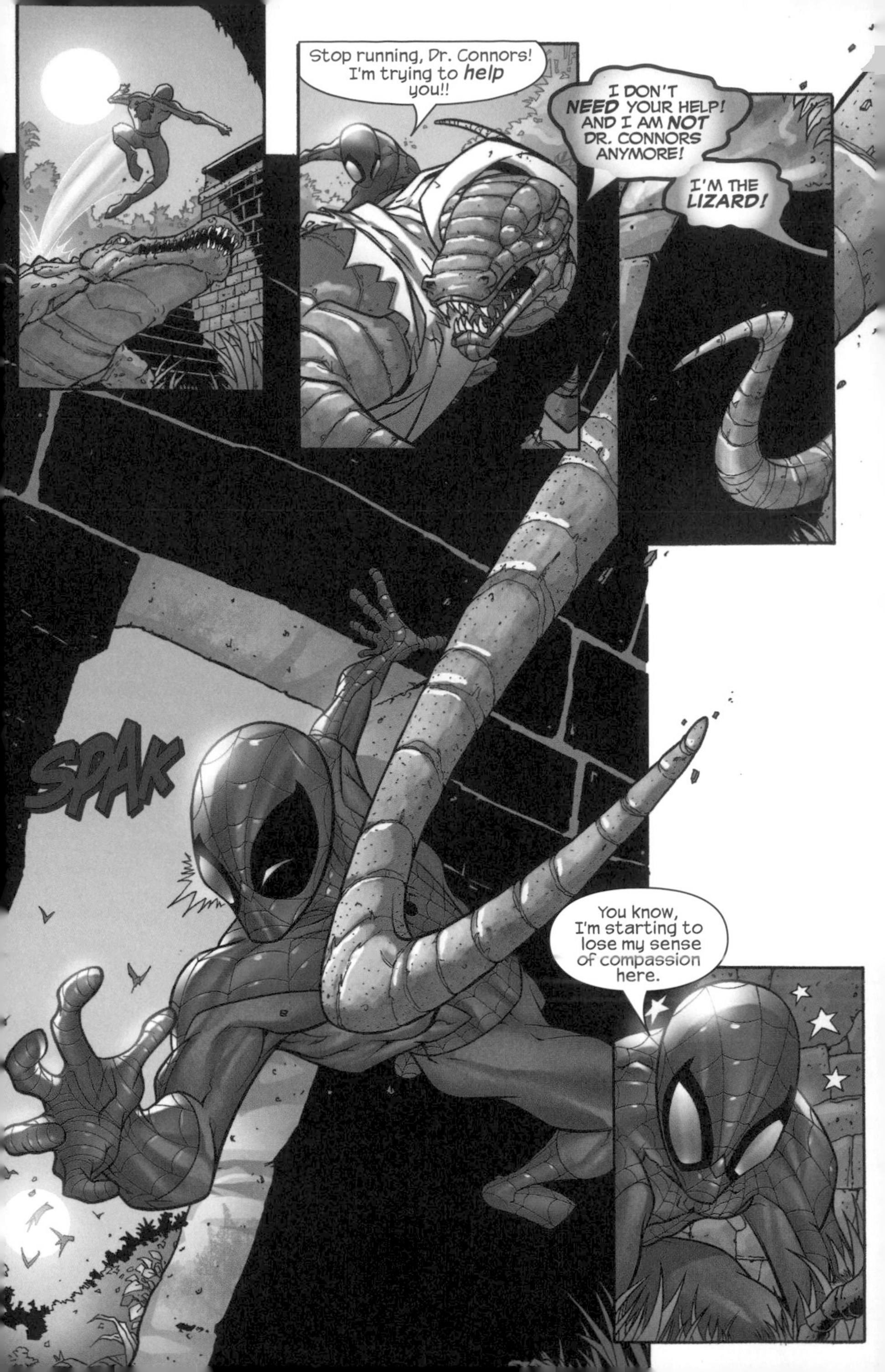
Stop running, Dr. Connors! I'm trying to help you!!
I DON'T NEED YOUR HELP! AND I AM NOT DR. CONNORS ANYMORE!
I'M THE LIZARD!
SPAK
You know, I'm starting to lose my sense of compassion here.

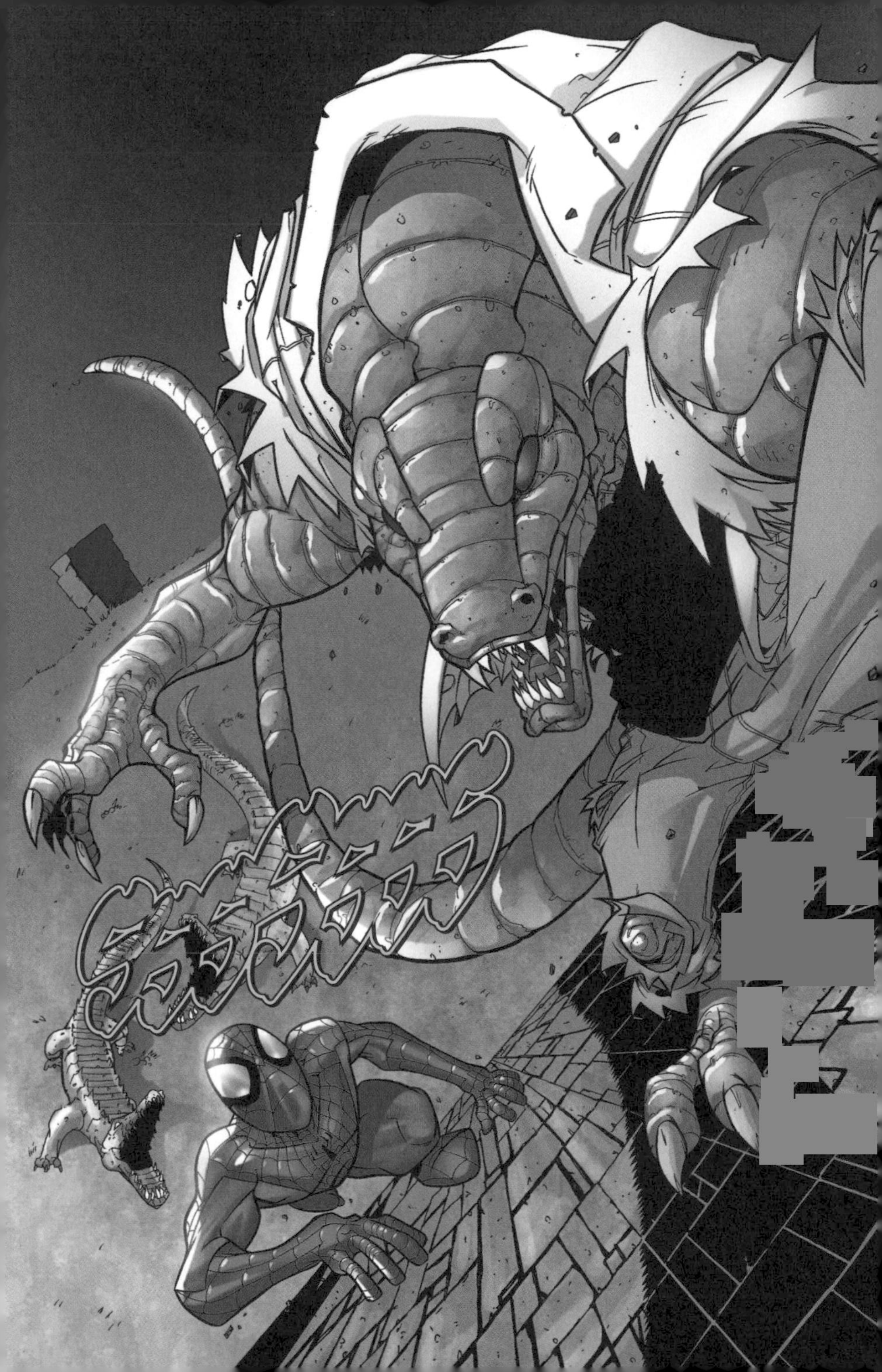

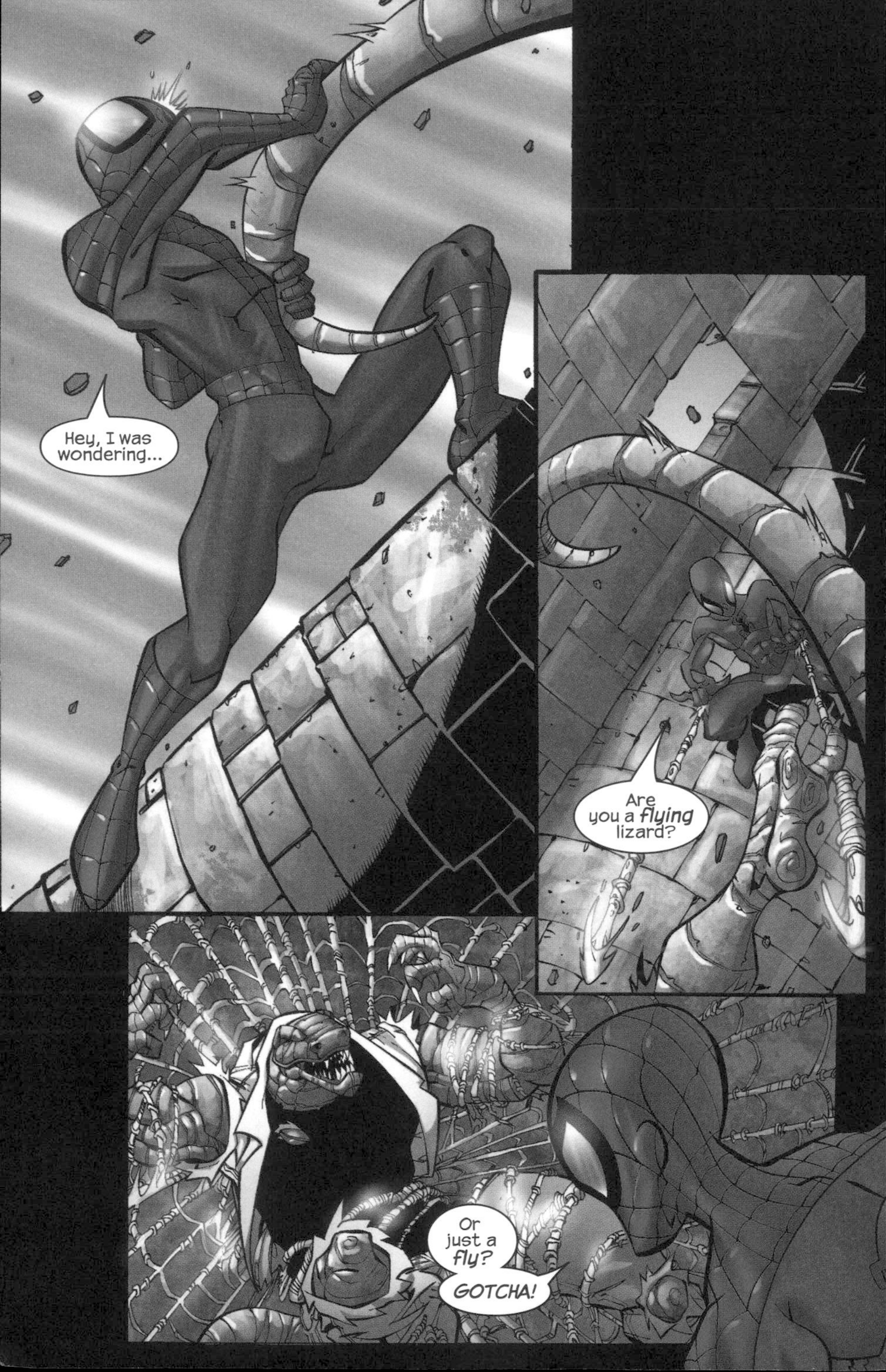
Hey, I was wondering...
Are you a *flying* lizard?
Or just a *fly*?
GOTCHA!

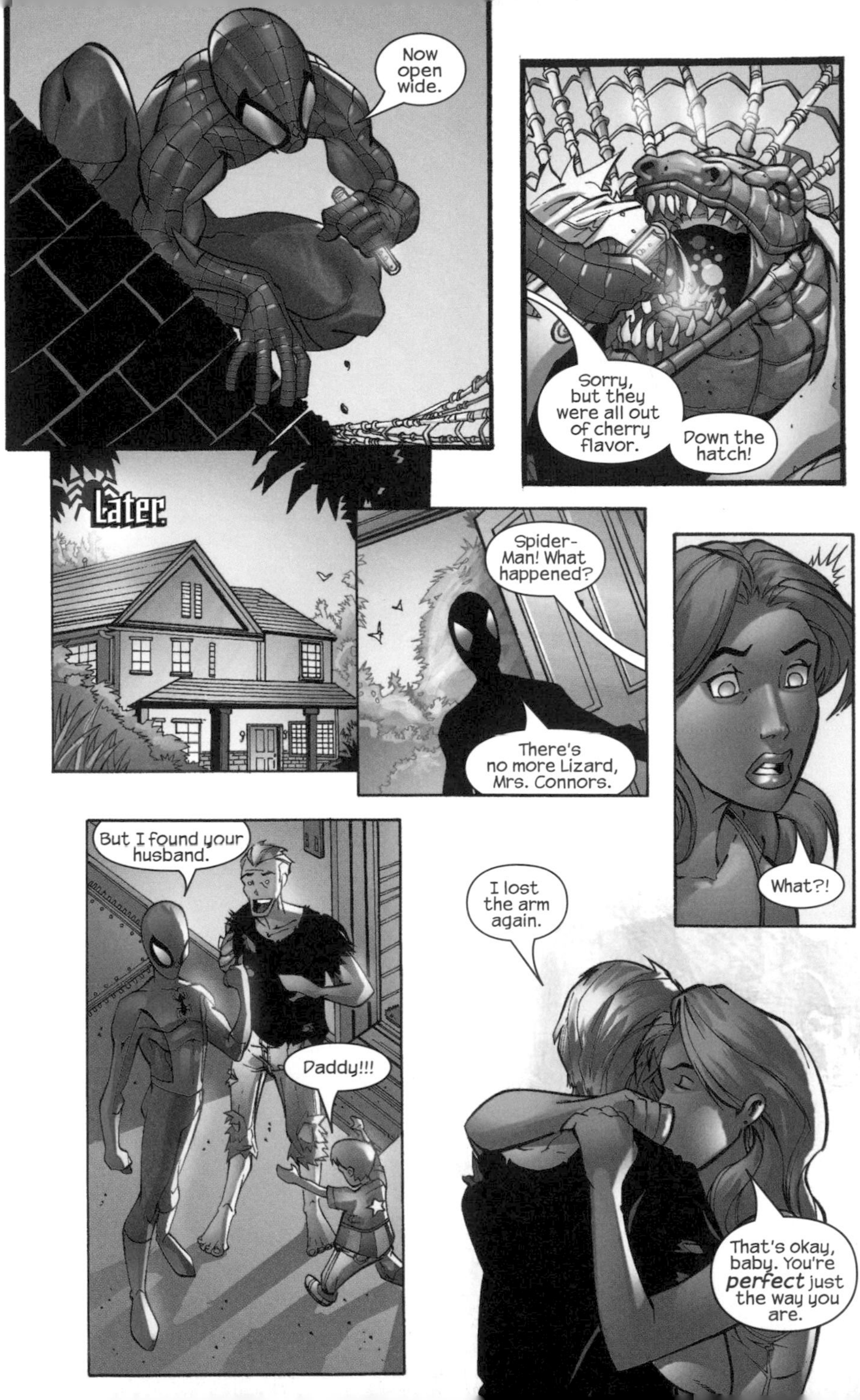
Now open wide.
Sorry, but they were all out of cherry flavor.
Down the hatch!
Later.
Spider-Man! What happened?
There's no more Lizard, Mrs. Connors.
What?!
But I found your husband.
Daddy!!!
I lost the arm again.
That's okay, baby. You're *perfect* just the way you are.

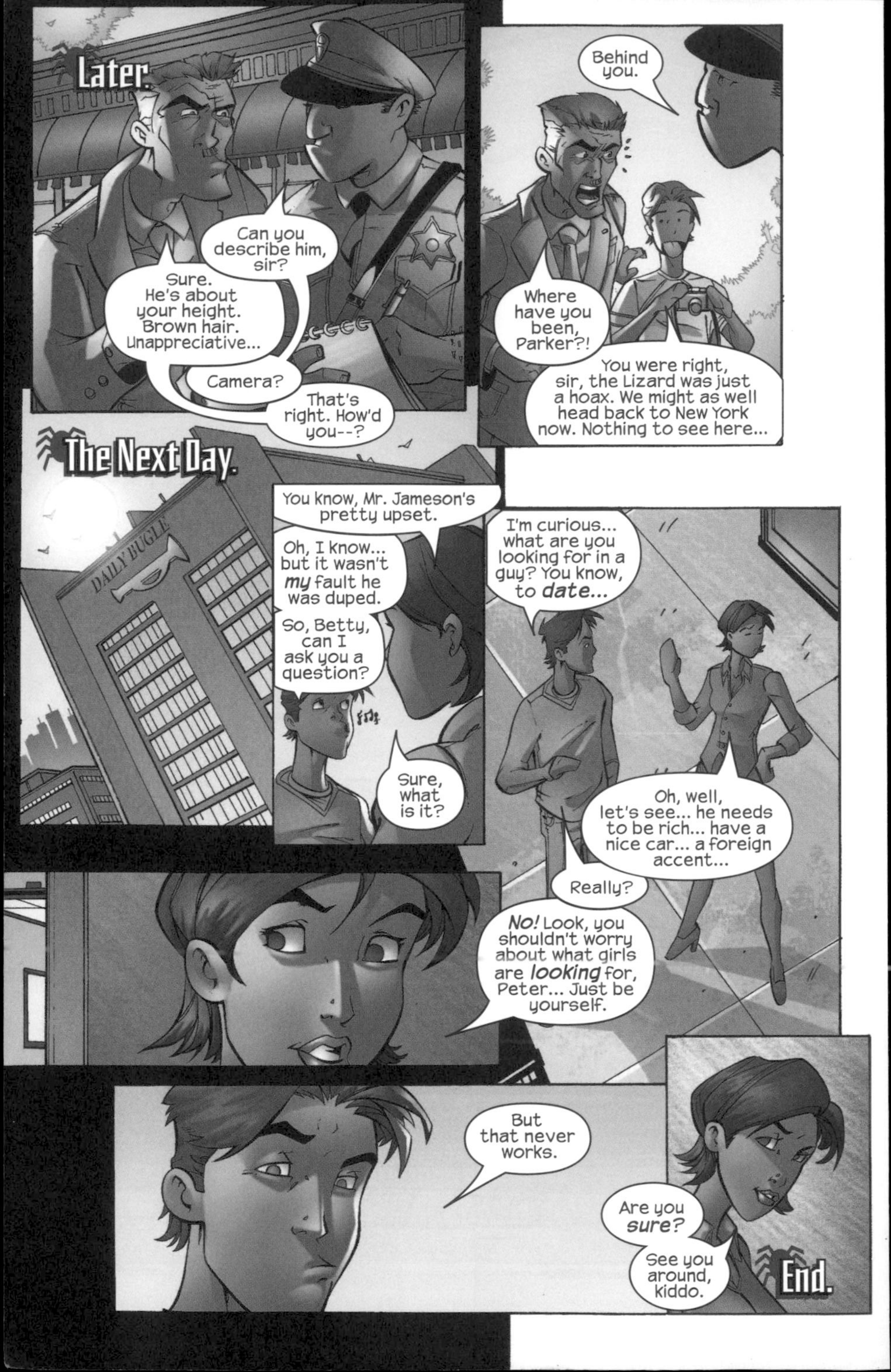
Later.
Can you describe him, sir?
Sure. He's about your height. Brown hair. Unappreciative...
Camera?
That's right. How'd you--?
Behind you.
Where have you been, Parker?!
You were right, sir, the Lizard was just a hoax. We might as well head back to New York now. Nothing to see here...
The Next Day.
DAILY BUGLE
You know, Mr. Jameson's pretty upset.
Oh, I know... but it wasn't *my* fault he was duped.
So, Betty, can I ask you a question?
Sure, what is it?
I'm curious... what are you looking for in a guy? You know, to ***date...***
Oh, well, let's see... he needs to be rich... have a nice car... a foreign accent...
Really?
No! Look, you shouldn't worry about what girls are ***looking*** for, Peter... Just be yourself.
But that never works.
Are you ***sure?***
See you around, kiddo.
End.

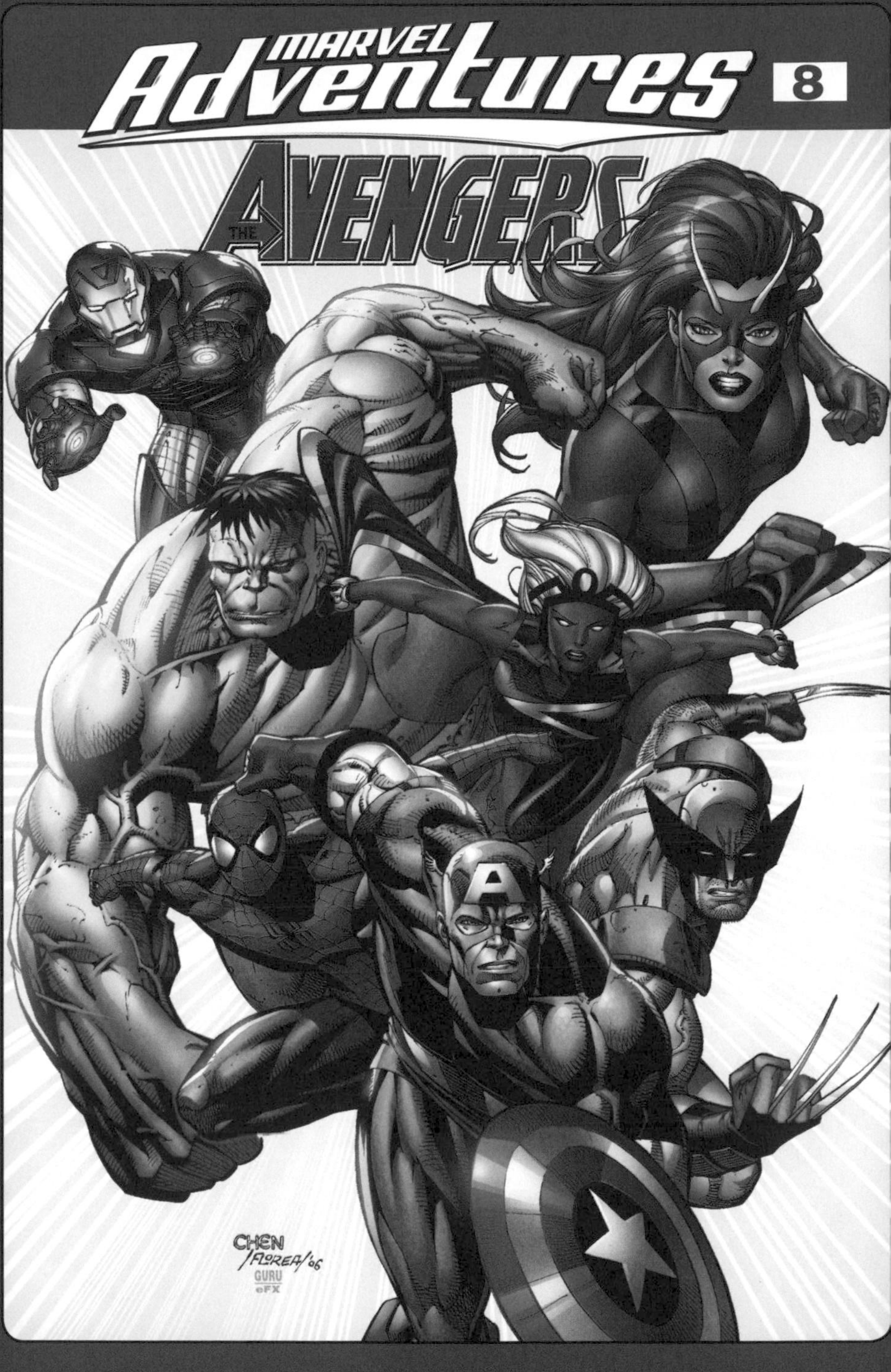

MARVEL Adventures
8
THE AVENGERS
CHEN /FLOREA/'06
GURU eFX

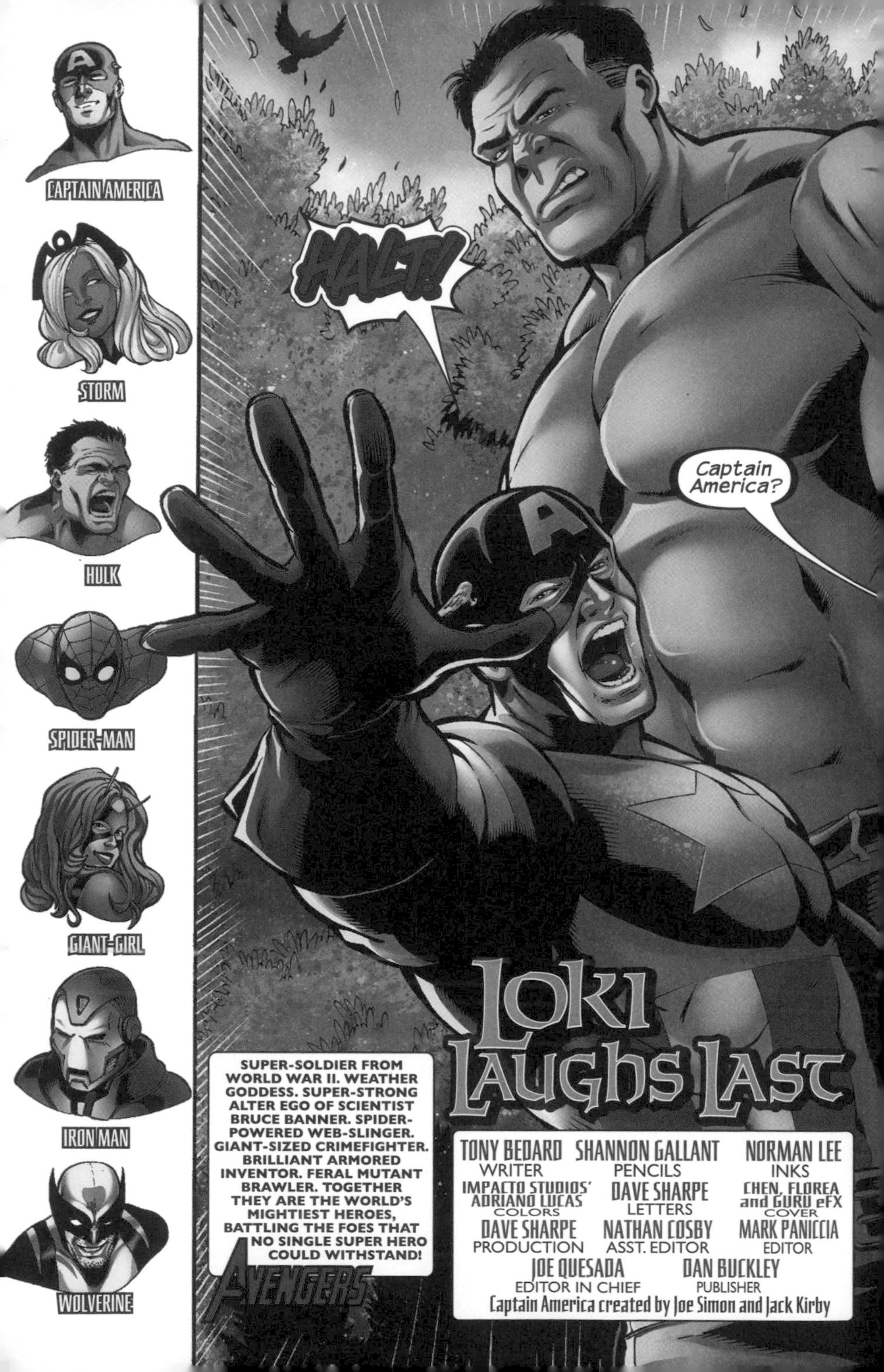
CAPTAIN AMERICA
STORM
HULK
SPIDER-MAN
GIANT-GIRL
IRON MAN
WOLVERINE
HALT!
Captain America?
LOKI LAUGHS LAST
SUPER-SOLDIER FROM WORLD WAR II. WEATHER GODDESS. SUPER-STRONG ALTER EGO OF SCIENTIST BRUCE BANNER. SPIDER-POWERED WEB-SLINGER. GIANT-SIZED CRIMEFIGHTER. BRILLIANT ARMORED INVENTOR. FERAL MUTANT BRAWLER. TOGETHER THEY ARE THE WORLD'S MIGHTIEST HEROES, BATTLING THE FOES THAT NO SINGLE SUPER HERO COULD WITHSTAND!
AVENGERS
TONY BEDARD WRITER
SHANNON GALLANT PENCILS
NORMAN LEE INKS
IMPACTO STUDIOS' ADRIANO LUCAS COLORS
DAVE SHARPE LETTERS
CHEN, FLOREA and GURU eFX COVER
DAVE SHARPE PRODUCTION
NATHAN COSBY ASST. EDITOR
MARK PANICCIA EDITOR
JOE QUESADA EDITOR IN CHIEF
DAN BUCKLEY PUBLISHER
Captain America created by Joe Simon and Jack Kirby

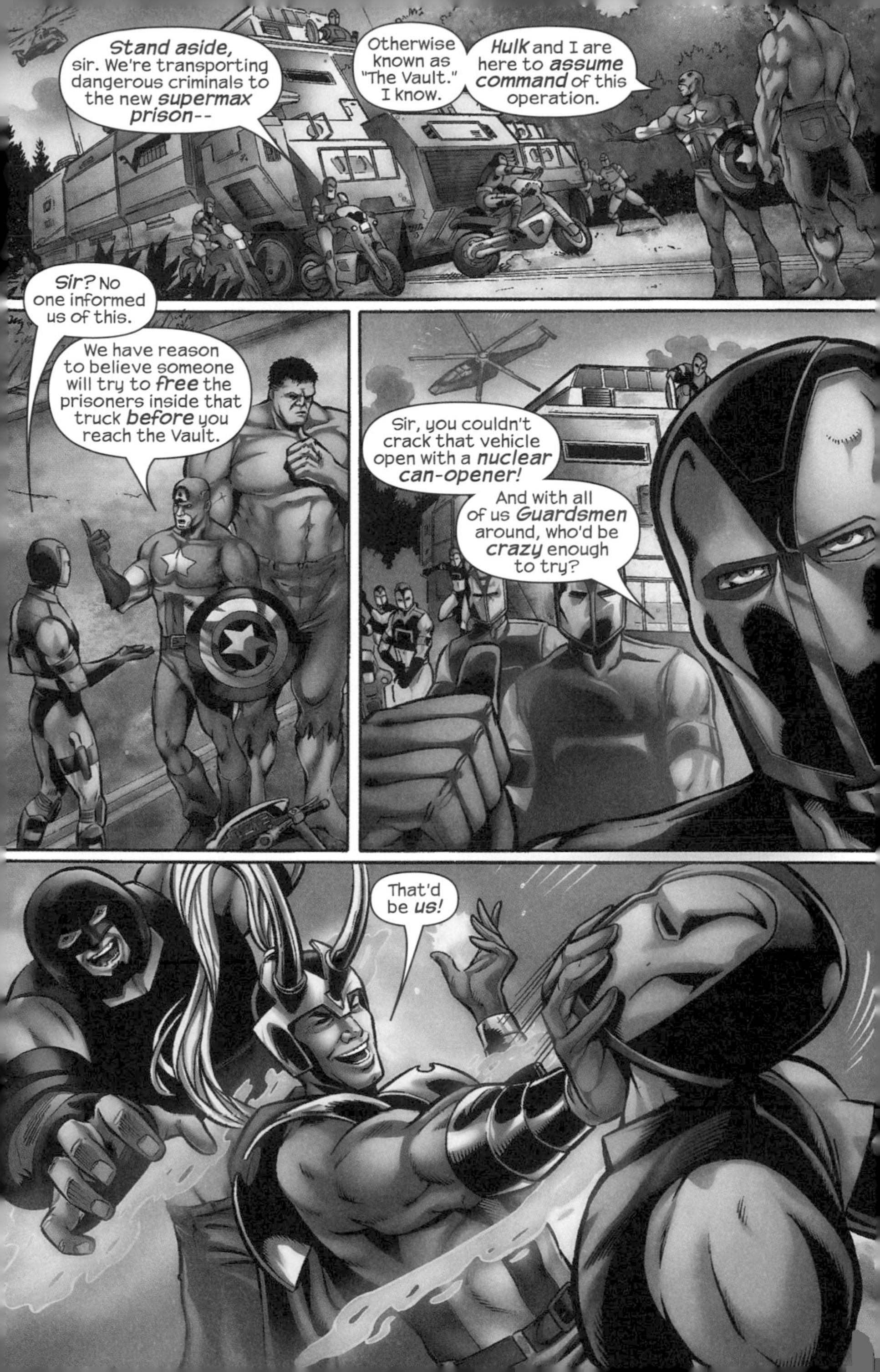
Stand aside, sir. We're transporting dangerous criminals to the new supermax prison--
Otherwise known as "The Vault." I know.
Hulk and I are here to assume command of this operation.
Sir? No one informed us of this.
We have reason to believe someone will try to free the prisoners inside that truck before you reach the Vault.
Sir, you couldn't crack that vehicle open with a nuclear can-opener!
And with all of us Guardsmen around, who'd be crazy enough to try?
That'd be us!

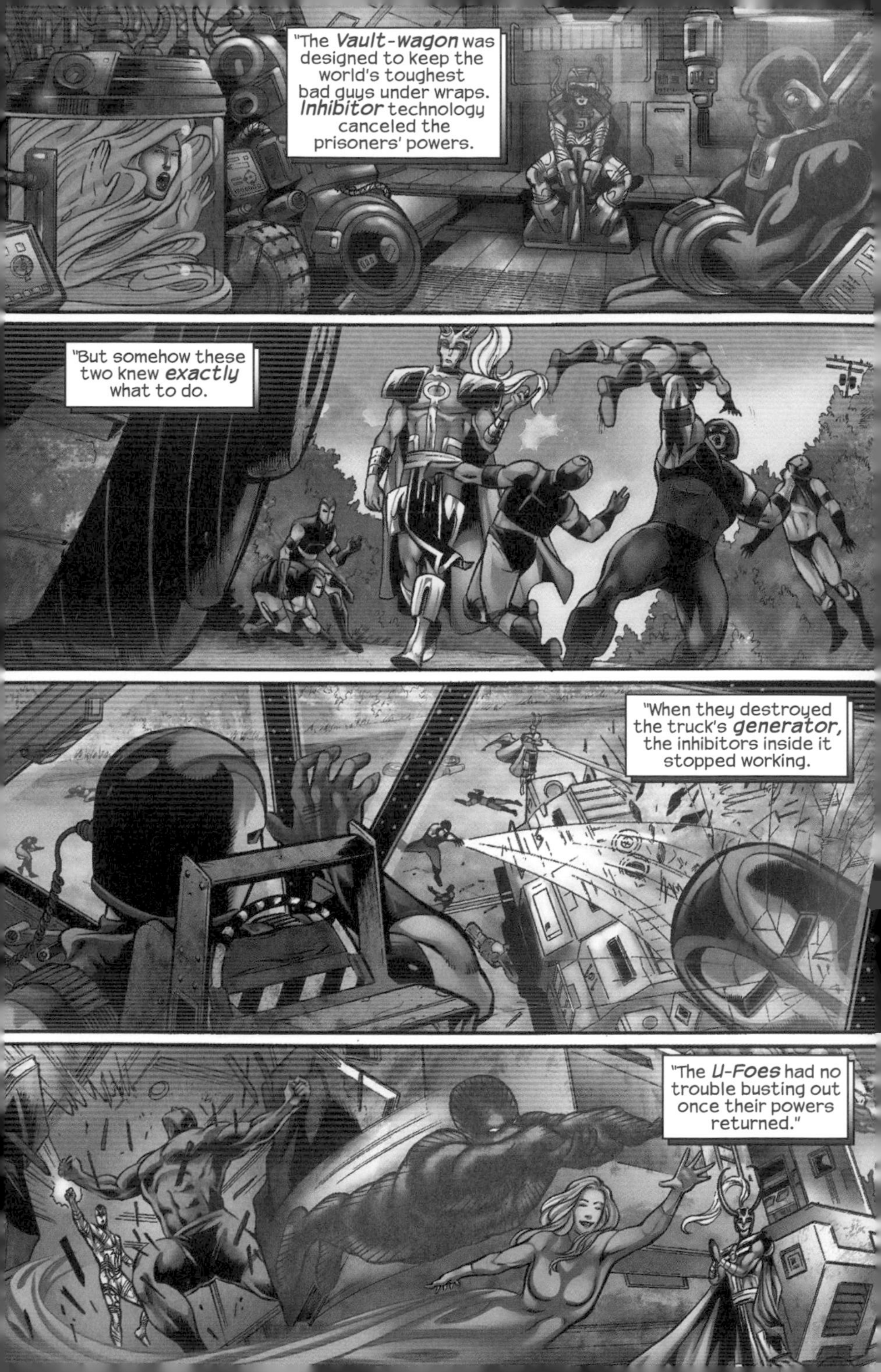
"The Vault-wagon was designed to keep the world's toughest bad guys under wraps. Inhibitor technology canceled the prisoners' powers.
"But somehow these two knew exactly what to do.
"When they destroyed the truck's generator, the inhibitors inside it stopped working.
"The U-Foes had no trouble busting out once their powers returned."

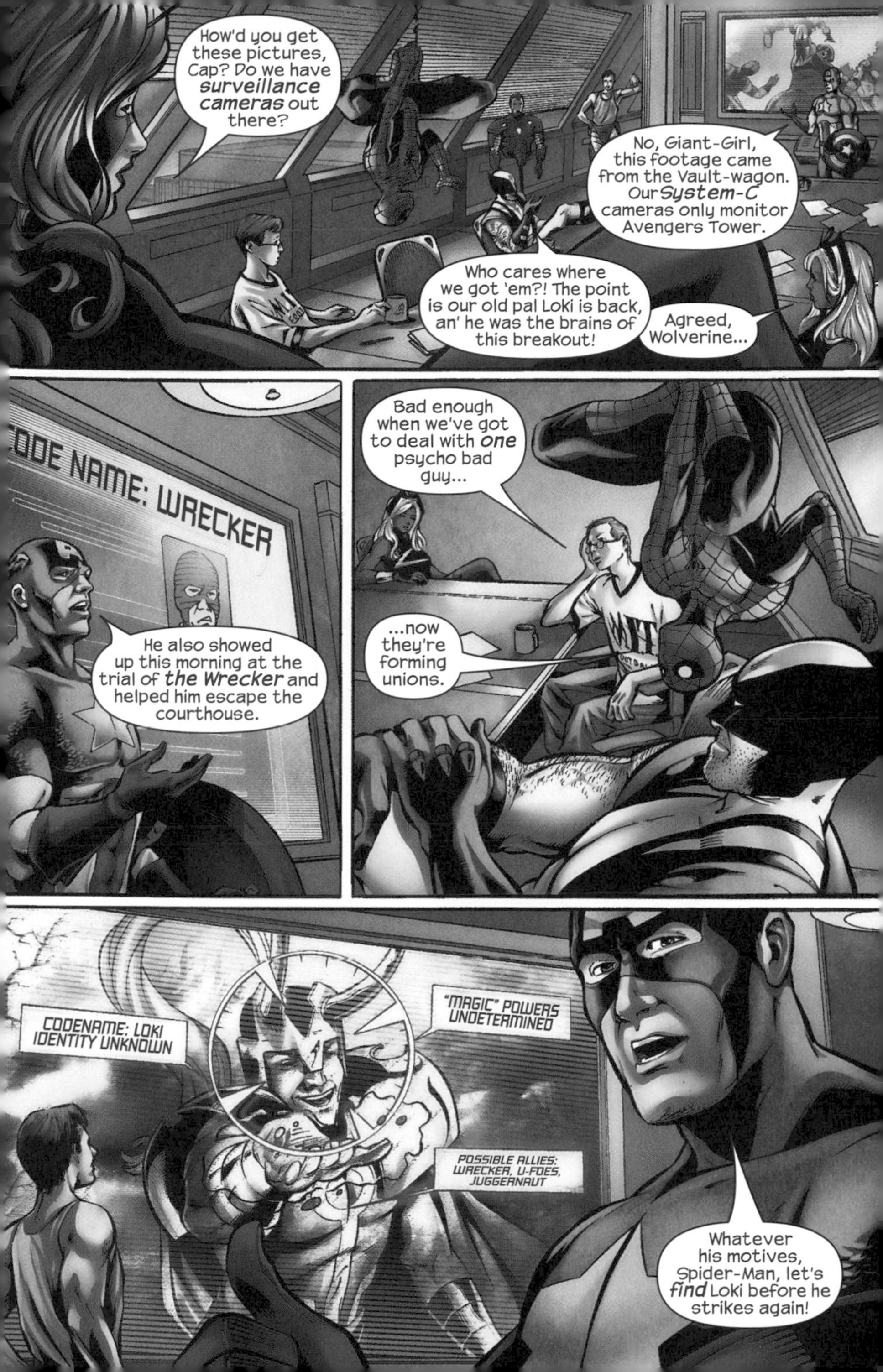
How'd you get these pictures, Cap? Do we have surveillance cameras out there?
No, Giant-Girl, this footage came from the Vault-wagon. Our System-C cameras only monitor Avengers Tower.
Who cares where we got 'em?! The point is our old pal Loki is back, an' he was the brains of this breakout!
Agreed, Wolverine...
CODE NAME: WRECKER
He also showed up this morning at the trial of the Wrecker and helped him escape the courthouse.
Bad enough when we've got to deal with one psycho bad guy...
...now they're forming unions.
CODENAME: LOKI IDENTITY UNKNOWN
"MAGIC" POWERS UNDETERMINED
POSSIBLE ALLIES: WRECKER, U-FOES, JUGGERNAUT
Whatever his motives, Spider-Man, let's find Loki before he strikes again!

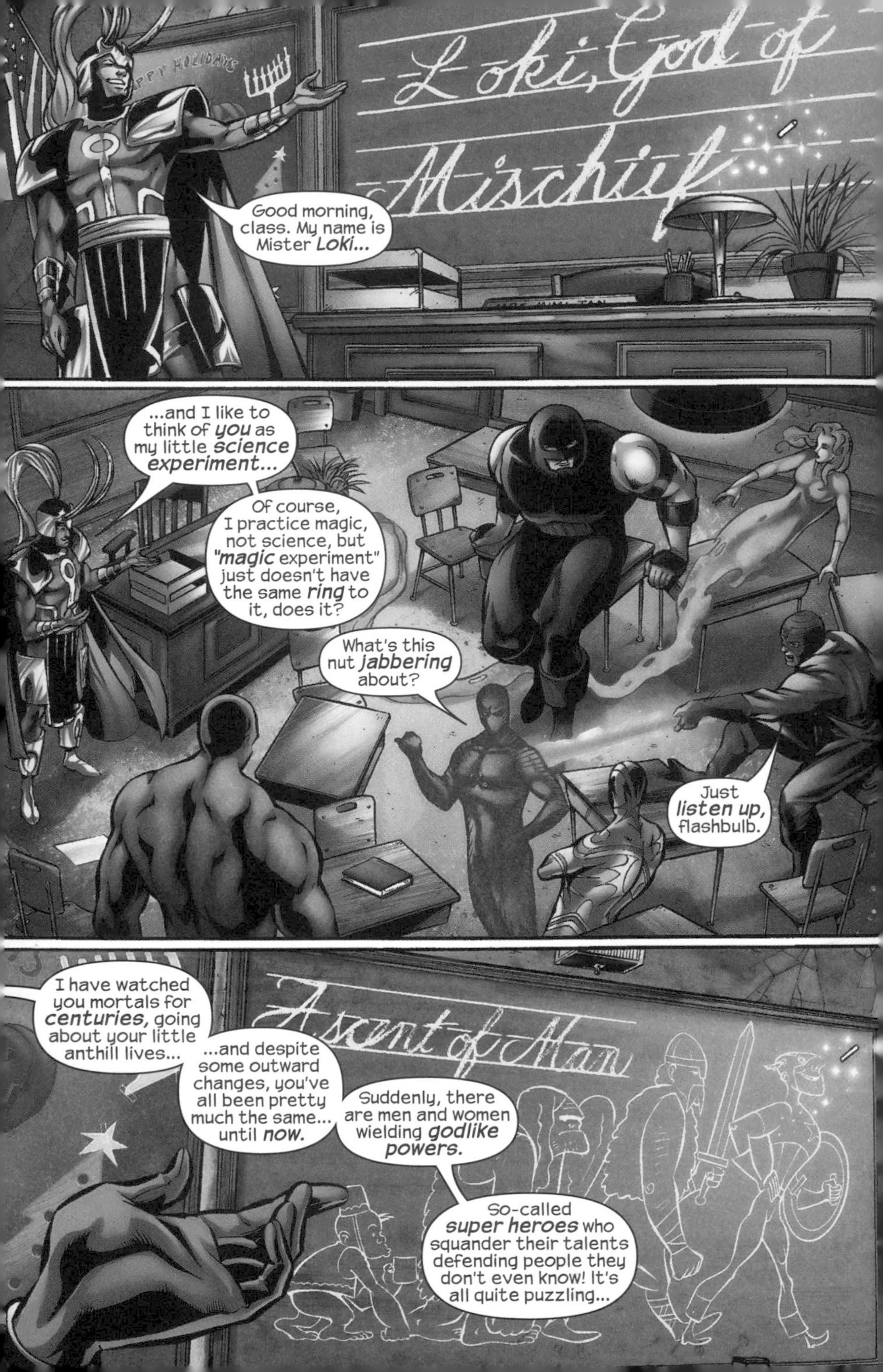
PPY HOLIDAYS
Loki, God of Mischief
Good morning, class. My name is Mister Loki...
...and I like to think of you as my little science experiment...
Of course, I practice magic, not science, but "magic experiment" just doesn't have the same ring to it, does it?
What's this nut jabbering about?
Just listen up, flashbulb.
Ascent of Man
I have watched you mortals for centuries, going about your little anthill lives...
...and despite some outward changes, you've all been pretty much the same... until now.
Suddenly, there are men and women wielding godlike powers.
So-called super heroes who squander their talents defending people they don't even know! It's all quite puzzling...

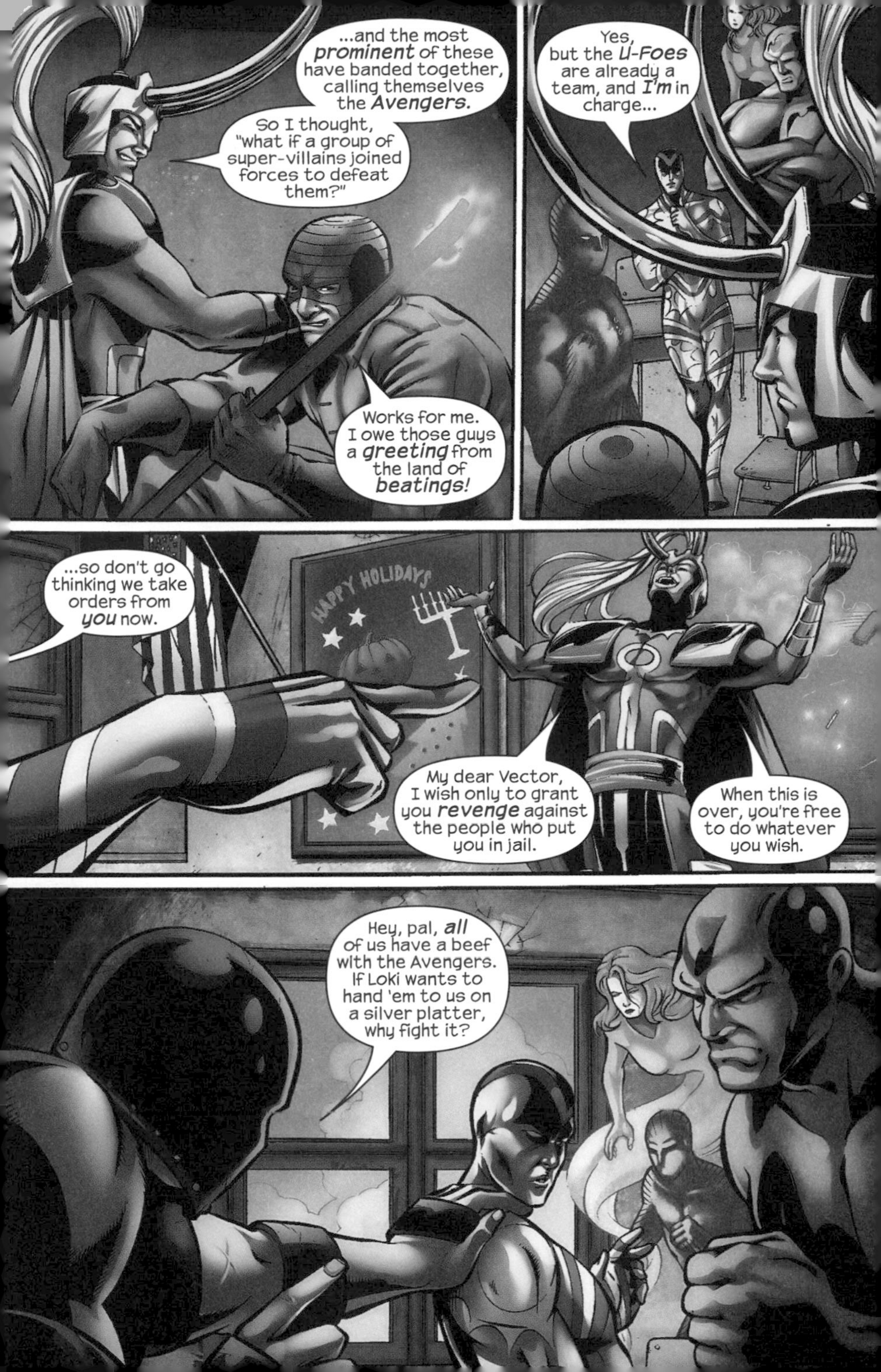
...and the most prominent of these have banded together, calling themselves the Avengers.
So I thought, "what if a group of super-villains joined forces to defeat them?"
Works for me. I owe those guys a greeting from the land of beatings!
Yes, but the U-Foes are already a team, and I'm in charge...
...so don't go thinking we take orders from you now.
HAPPY HOLIDAYS
My dear Vector, I wish only to grant you revenge against the people who put you in jail.
When this is over, you're free to do whatever you wish.
Hey, pal, all of us have a beef with the Avengers. If Loki wants to hand 'em to us on a silver platter, why fight it?

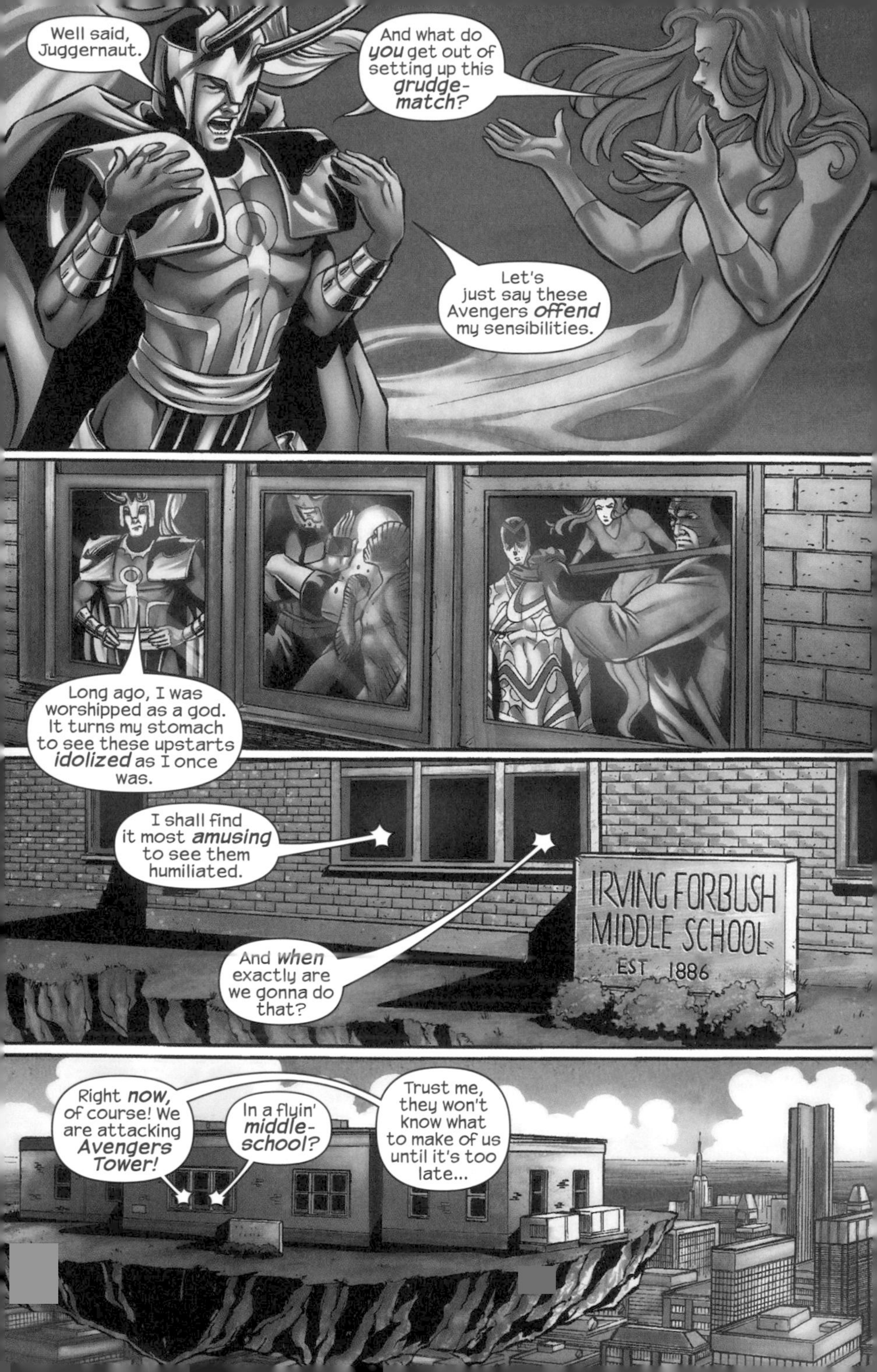
Well said, Juggernaut.
And what do you get out of setting up this grudge-match?
Let's just say these Avengers offend my sensibilities.
Long ago, I was worshipped as a god. It turns my stomach to see these upstarts idolized as I once was.
I shall find it most amusing to see them humiliated.
IRVING FORBUSH MIDDLE SCHOOL EST 1886
And when exactly are we gonna do that?
Right now, of course! We are attacking Avengers Tower!
In a flyin' middle-school?
Trust me, they won't know what to make of us until it's too late...

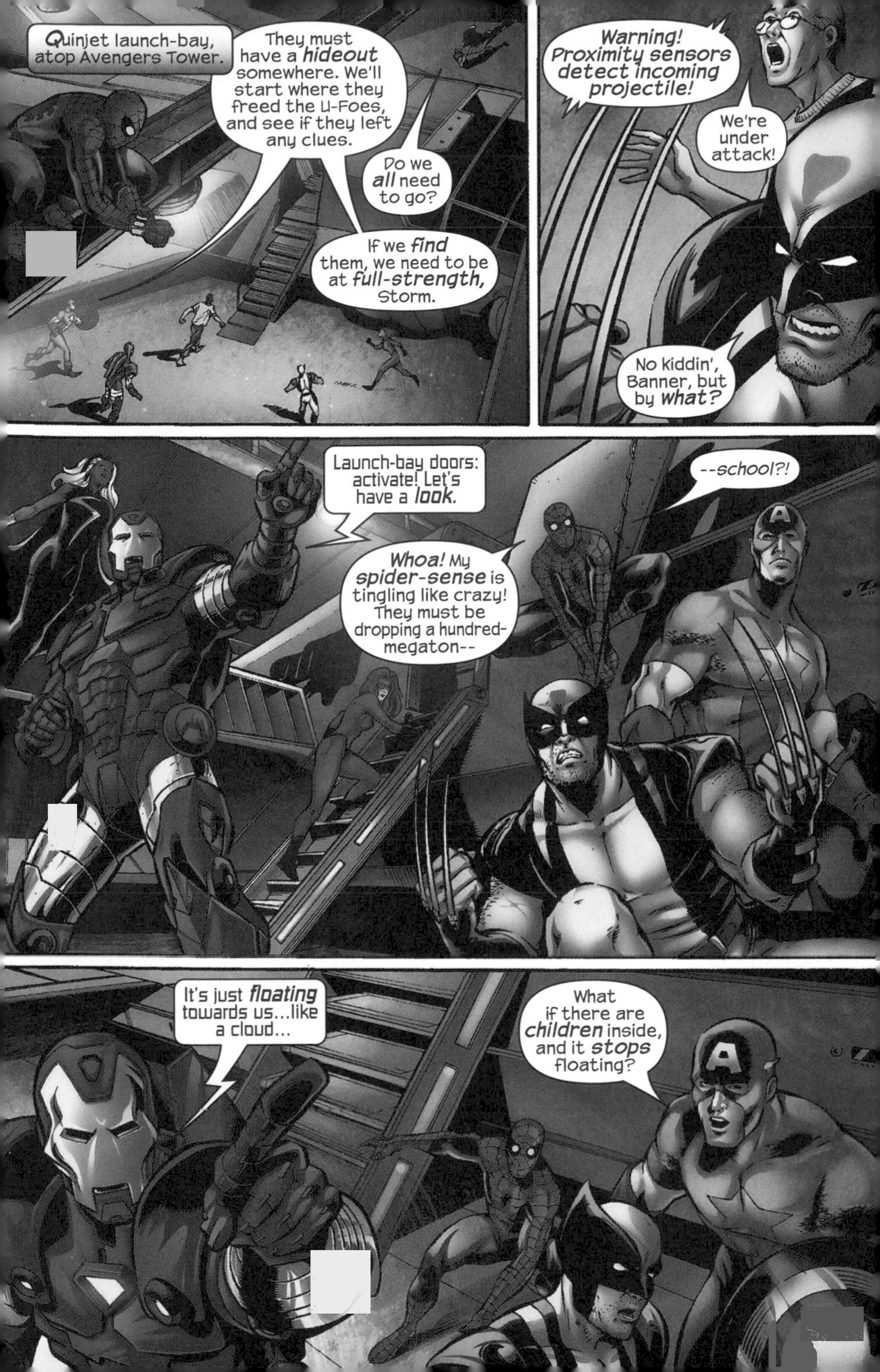

Quinjet launch-bay, atop Avengers Tower.
They must have a hideout somewhere. We'll start where they freed the U-Foes, and see if they left any clues.
Do we all need to go?
If we find them, we need to be at full-strength, Storm.
Warning! Proximity sensors detect incoming projectile!
We're under attack!
No kiddin', Banner, but by what?
Launch-bay doors: activate! Let's have a look.
Whoa! My spider-sense is tingling like crazy! They must be dropping a hundred-megaton--
--school?!
It's just floating towards us...like a cloud...
What if there are children inside, and it stops floating?

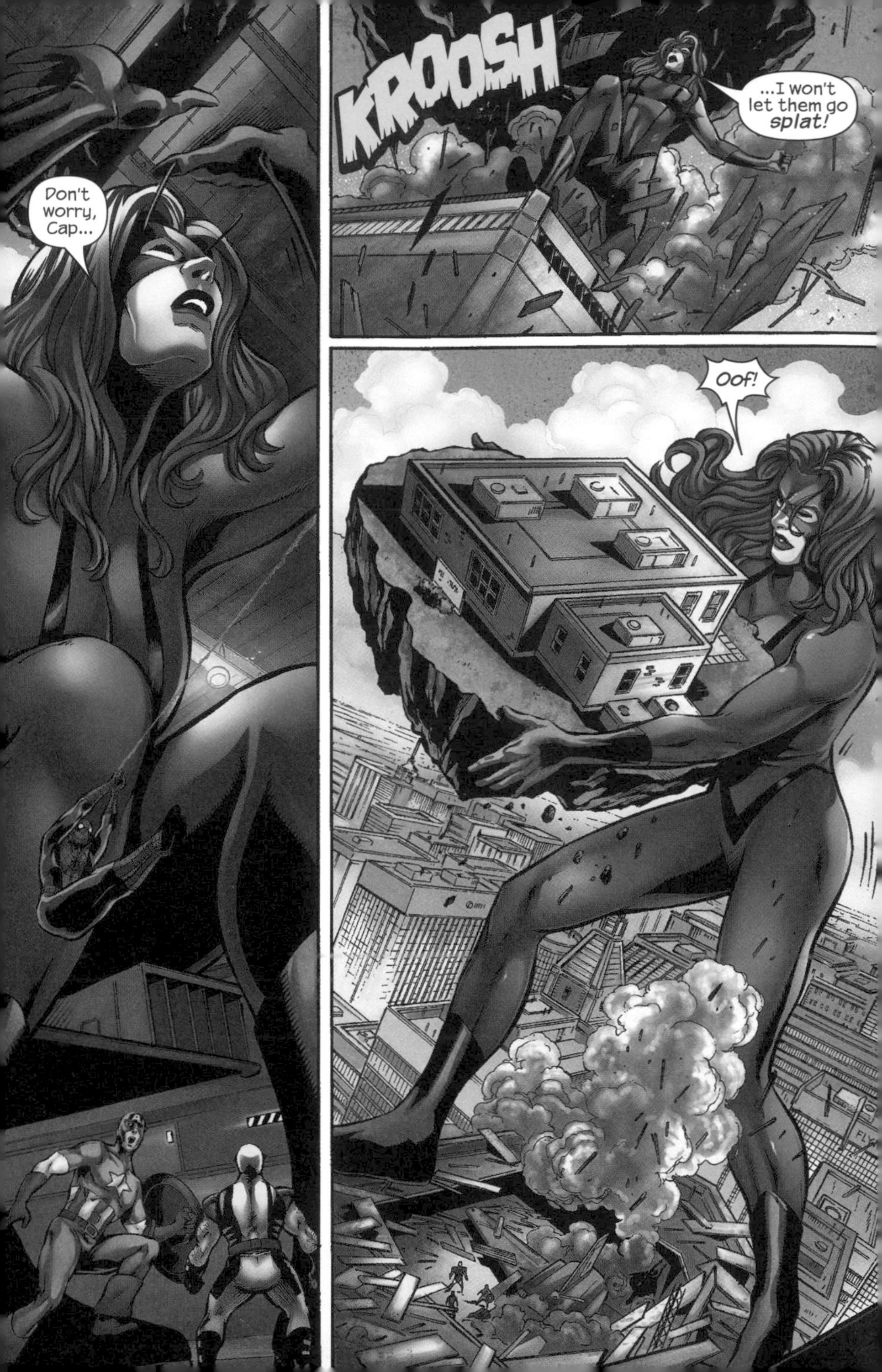
Don't worry, Cap...
KROOSH
...I won't let them go *splat!*
Oof!

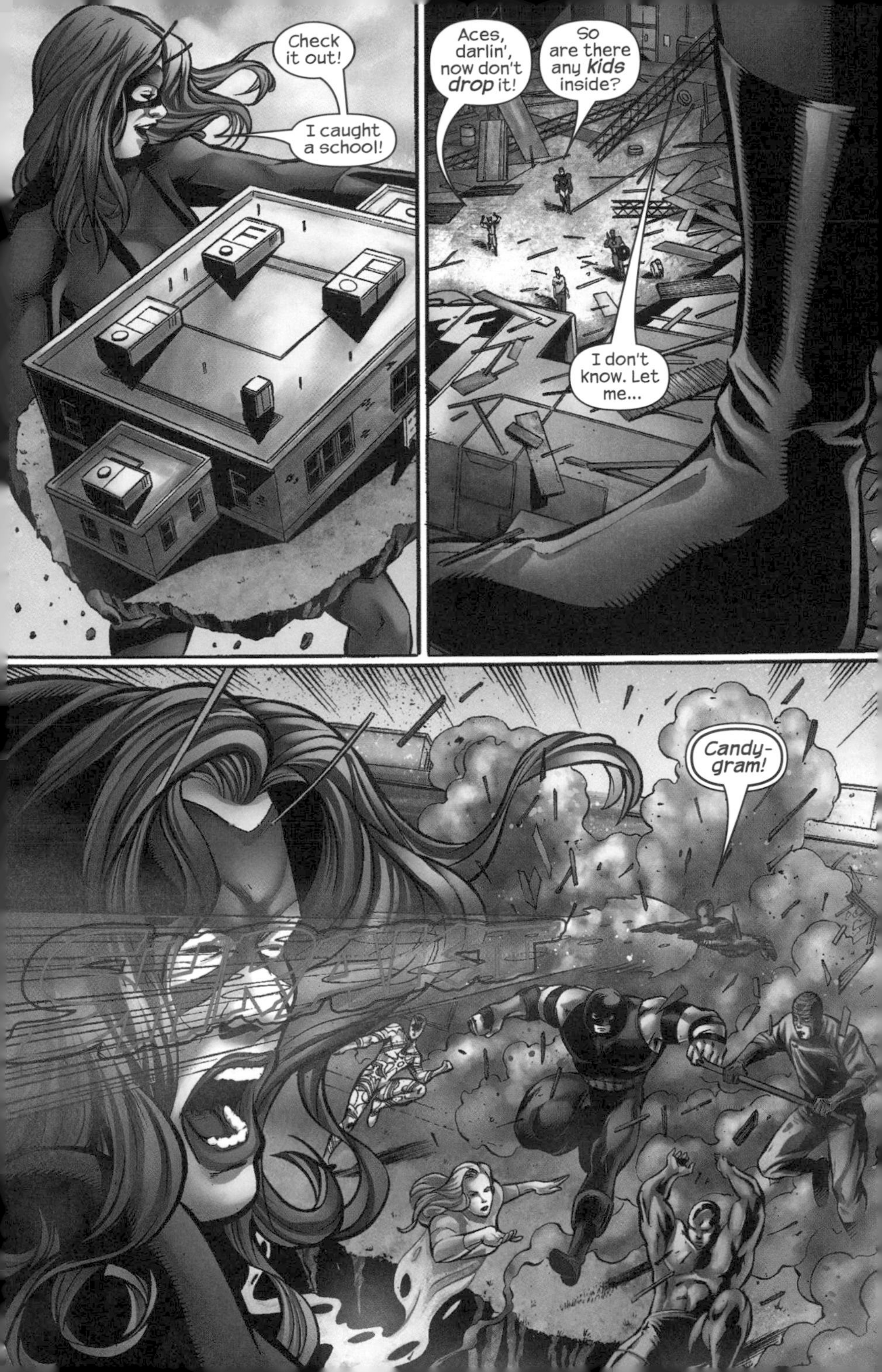
Check it out!
I caught a school!
Aces, darlin', now don't drop it!
So are there any kids inside?
I don't know. Let me...
Candy-gram!

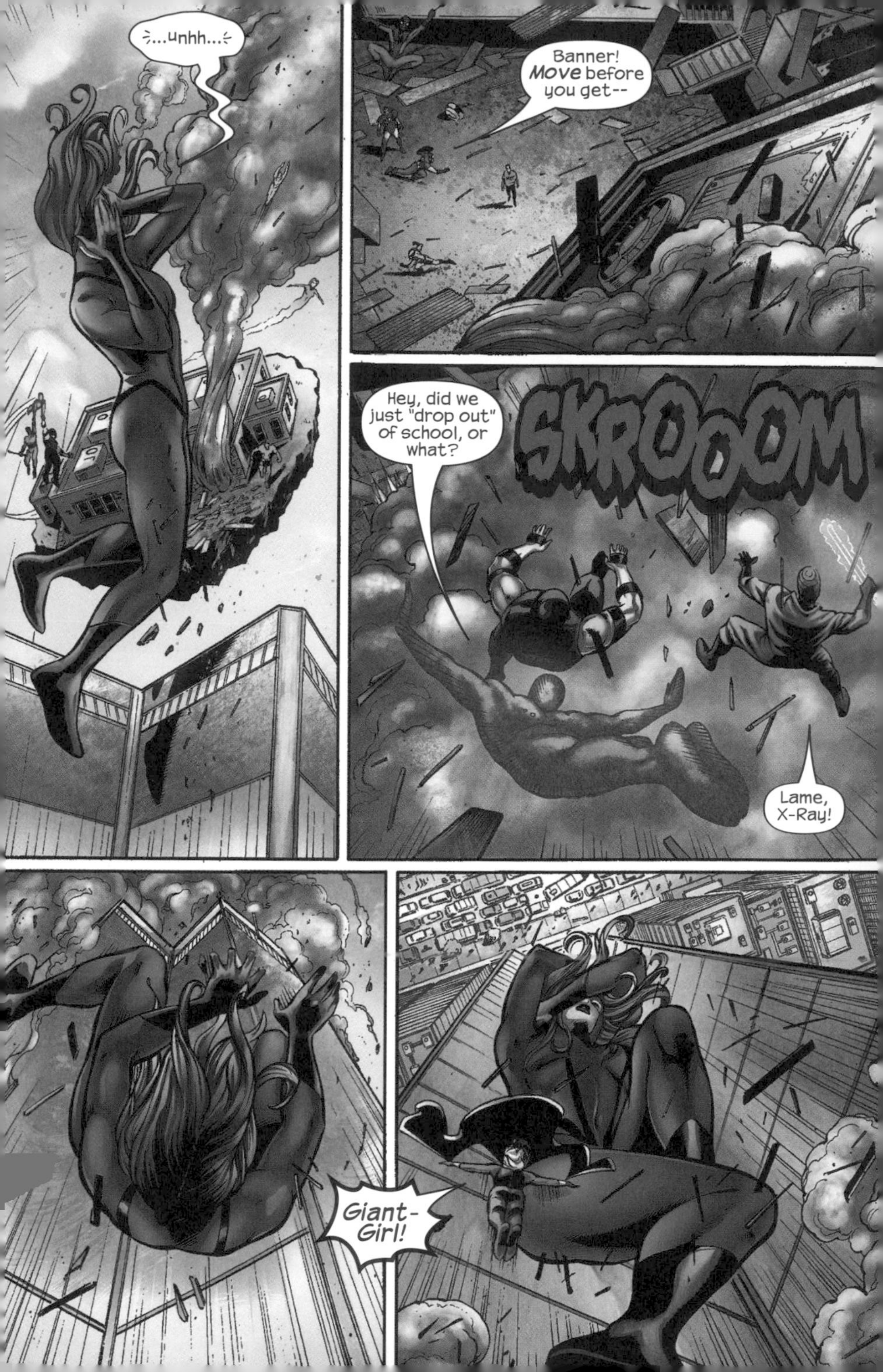
...unhh...
Banner! Move before you get--
Hey, did we just "drop out" of school, or what?
SKROOOM
Lame, X-Ray!
Giant-Girl!

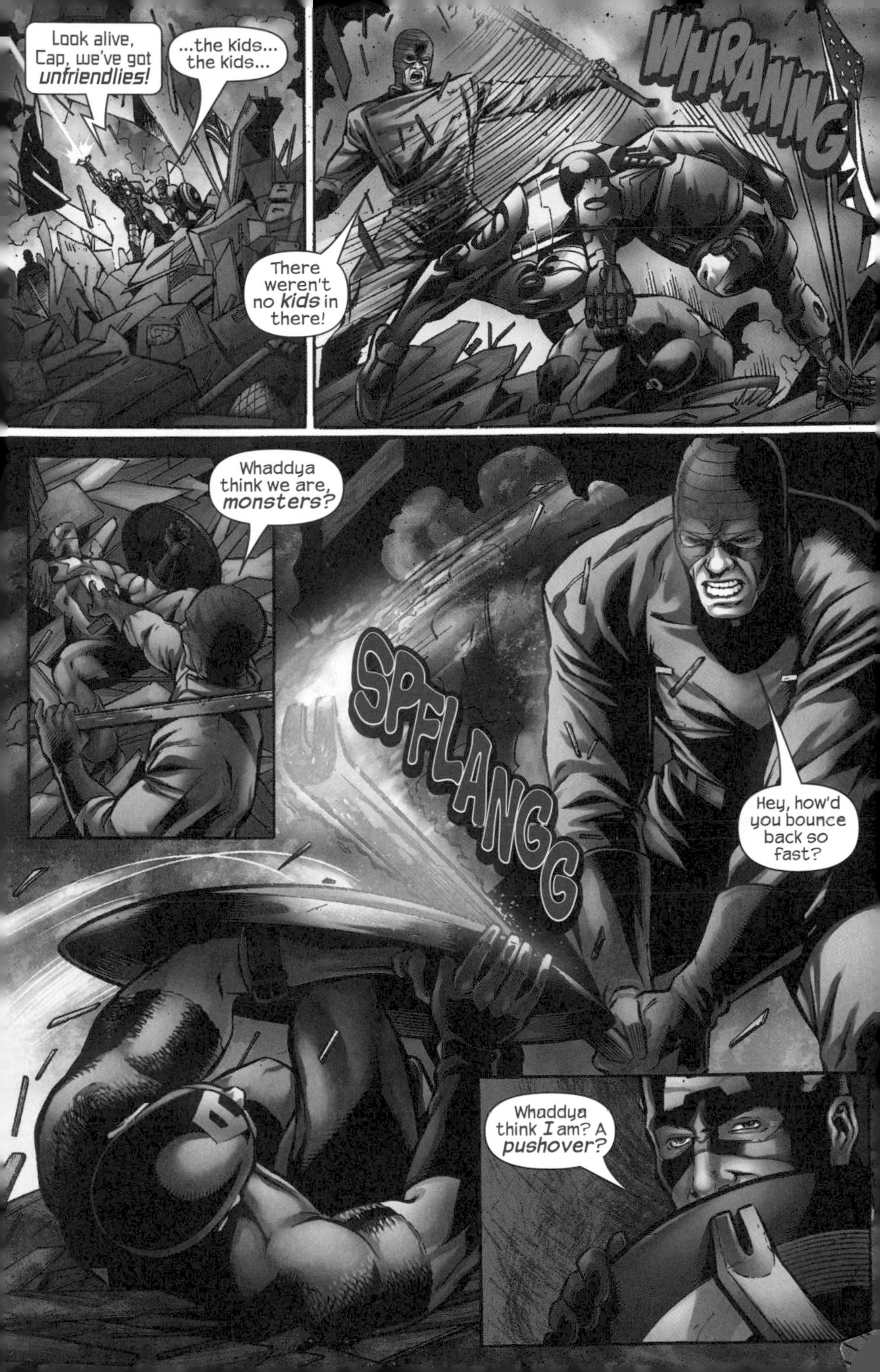
Look alive, Cap, we've got unfriendlies!
...the kids... the kids...
WHRANNG
There weren't no kids in there!
Whaddya think we are, monsters?
SPFLANGG
Hey, how'd you bounce back so fast?
Whaddya think I am? A pushover?

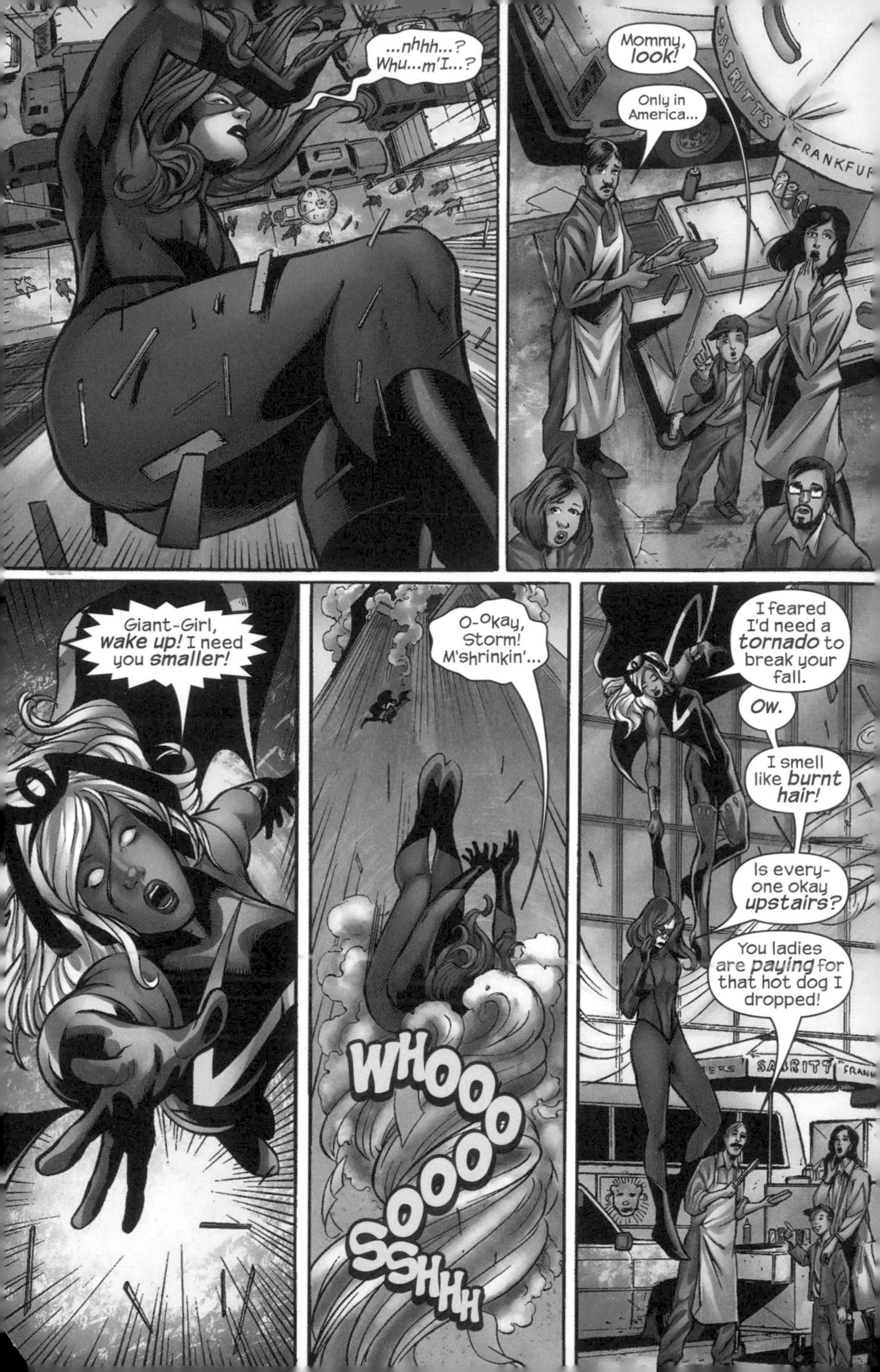
...nhhh...? Whu...m'I...?
Mommy, look!
Only in America...
SABRITTS
FRANKFUR
Giant-Girl, wake up! I need you smaller!
O-Okay, Storm! M'shrinkin'...
WHOOOO
SOOOO
SSHHH
I feared I'd need a tornado to break your fall.
Ow.
I smell like burnt hair!
Is every-one okay upstairs?
You ladies are paying for that hot dog I dropped!

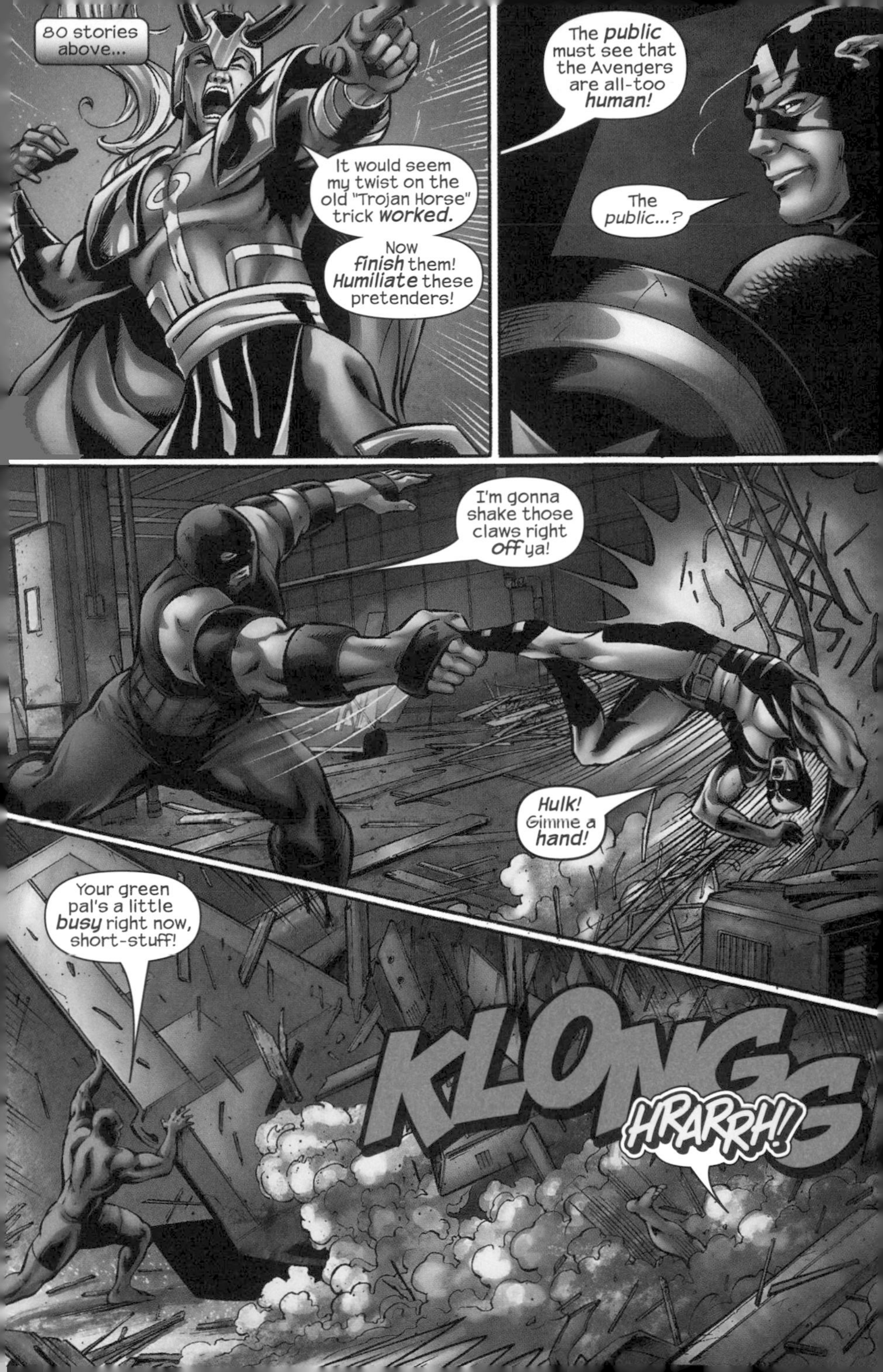
80 stories above...
It would seem my twist on the old "Trojan Horse" trick worked.
Now finish them! Humiliate these pretenders!
The public must see that the Avengers are all-too human!
The public...?
I'm gonna shake those claws right off ya!
Hulk! Gimme a hand!
Your green pal's a little busy right now, short-stuff!
KLONGG
HRARRH!!

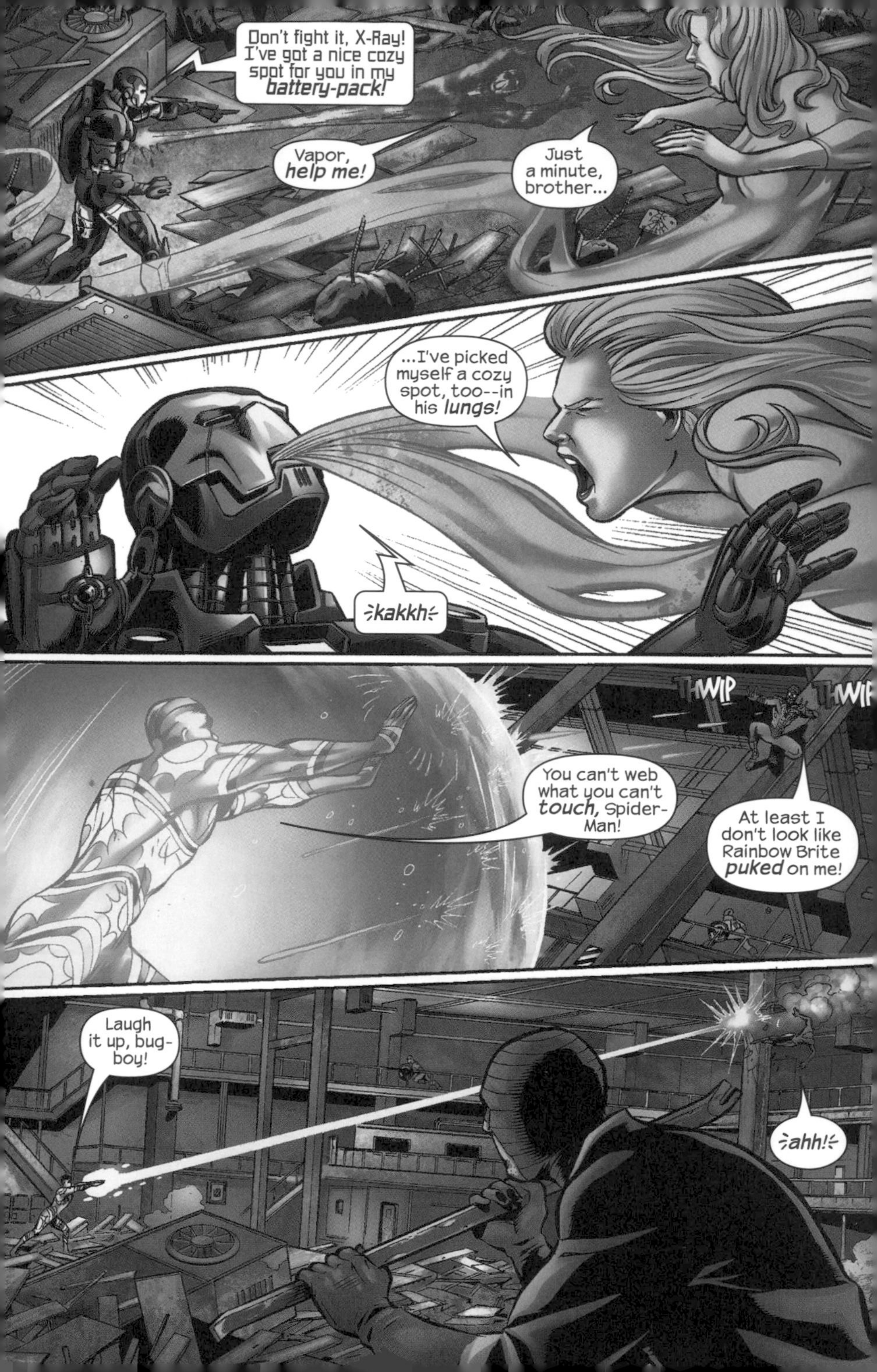

Don't fight it, X-Ray! I've got a nice cozy spot for you in my battery-pack!
Vapor, help me!
Just a minute, brother...
...I've picked myself a cozy spot, too--in his lungs!
kakkh
THWIP
THWIP
You can't web what you can't touch, Spider-Man!
At least I don't look like Rainbow Brite puked on me!
Laugh it up, bug-boy!
ahh!

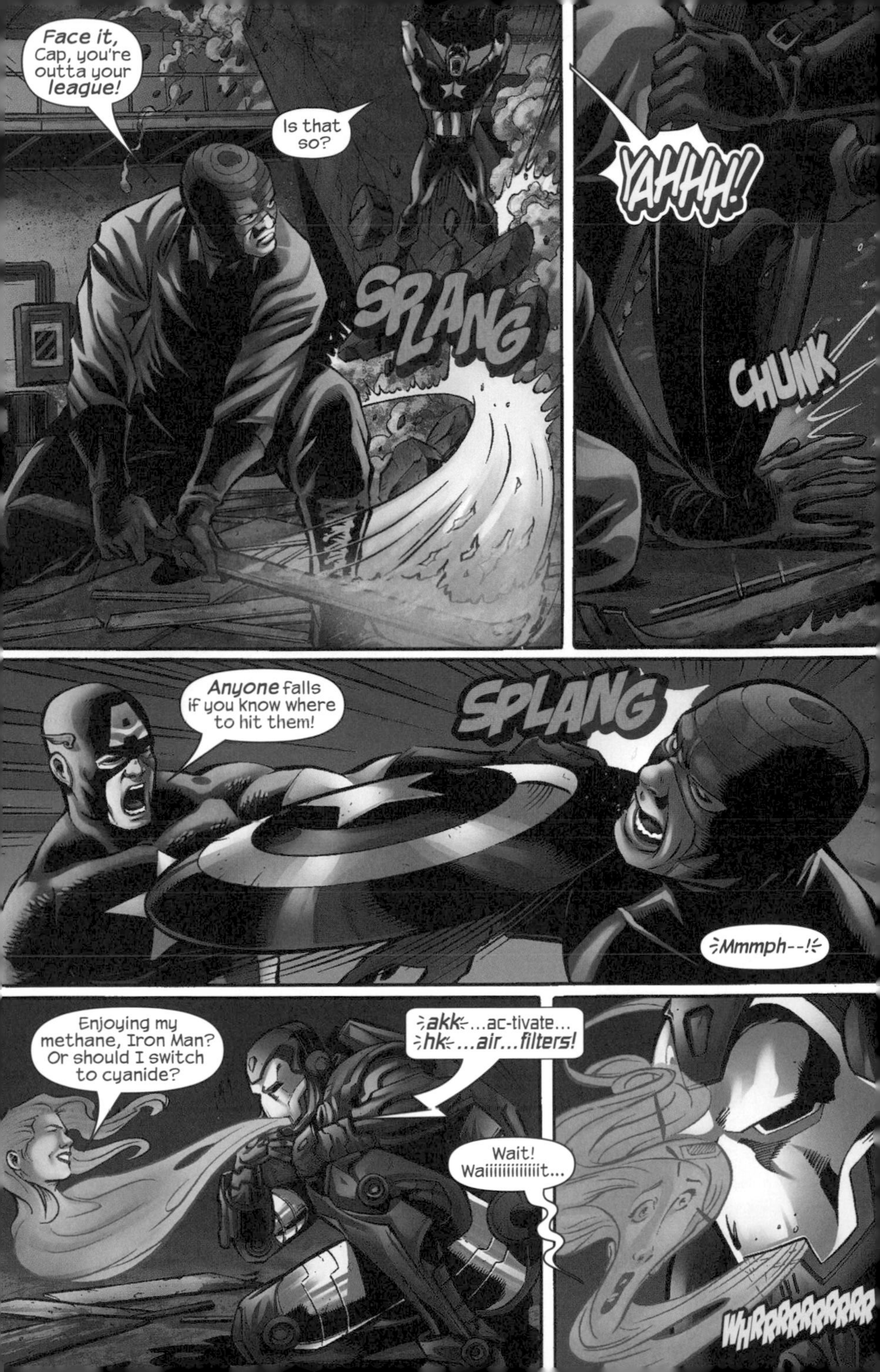

Face it, Cap, you're outta your league!
Is that so?
SPLANG
YAHHH!!
CHUNK
Anyone falls if you know where to hit them!
SPLANG
Mmmph--!
Enjoying my methane, Iron Man? Or should I switch to cyanide?
akk...ac-tivate... hk...air...filters!
Wait! Waiiiiiiiiiiiit...
WHRRRRRRRRRR

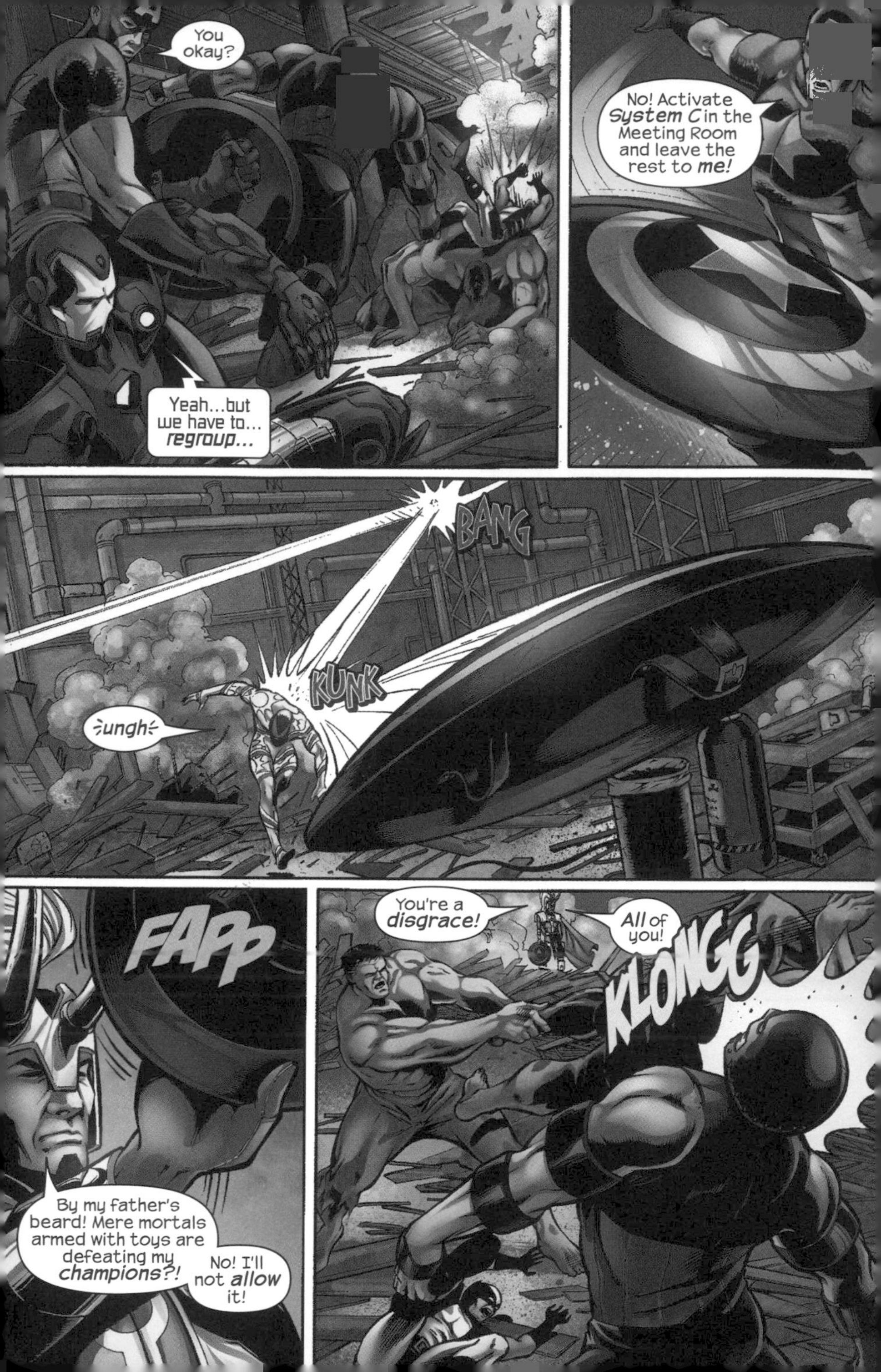
You okay?
Yeah...but we have to... *regroup...*
No! Activate *System C* in the Meeting Room and leave the rest to *me!*
BANG
KUNK
ungh
FAPP
By my father's beard! Mere mortals armed with toys are defeating my *champions?!*
No! I'll not *allow* it!
You're a *disgrace!*
All of you!
KLONGG

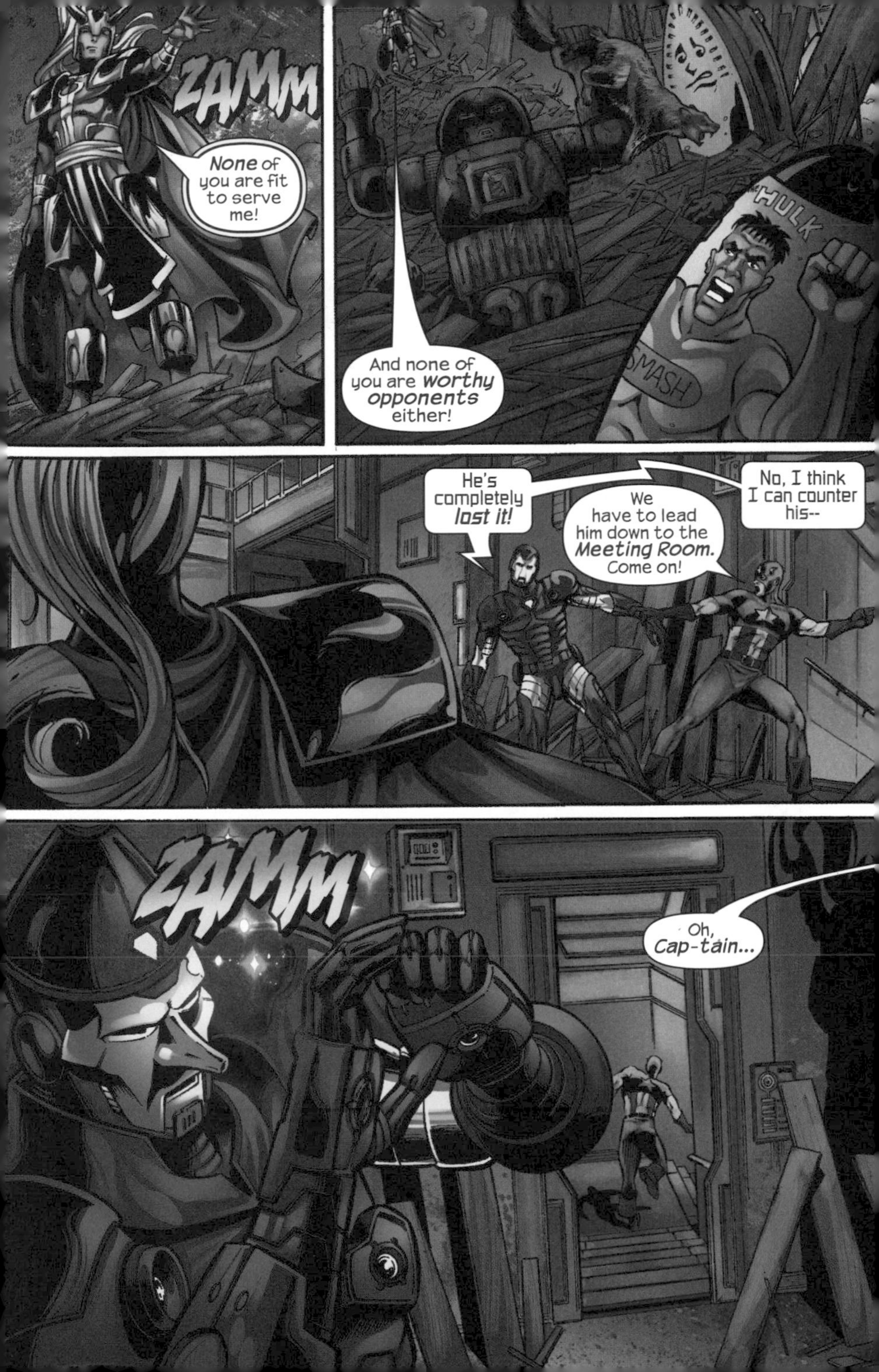

ZAMM
None of you are fit to serve me!
HULK
SMASH
And none of you are ***worthy opponents*** either!
He's completely ***lost it!***
We have to lead him down to the ***Meeting Room.*** Come on!
No, I think I can counter his--
ZAMM
Oh, *Cap-tain...*

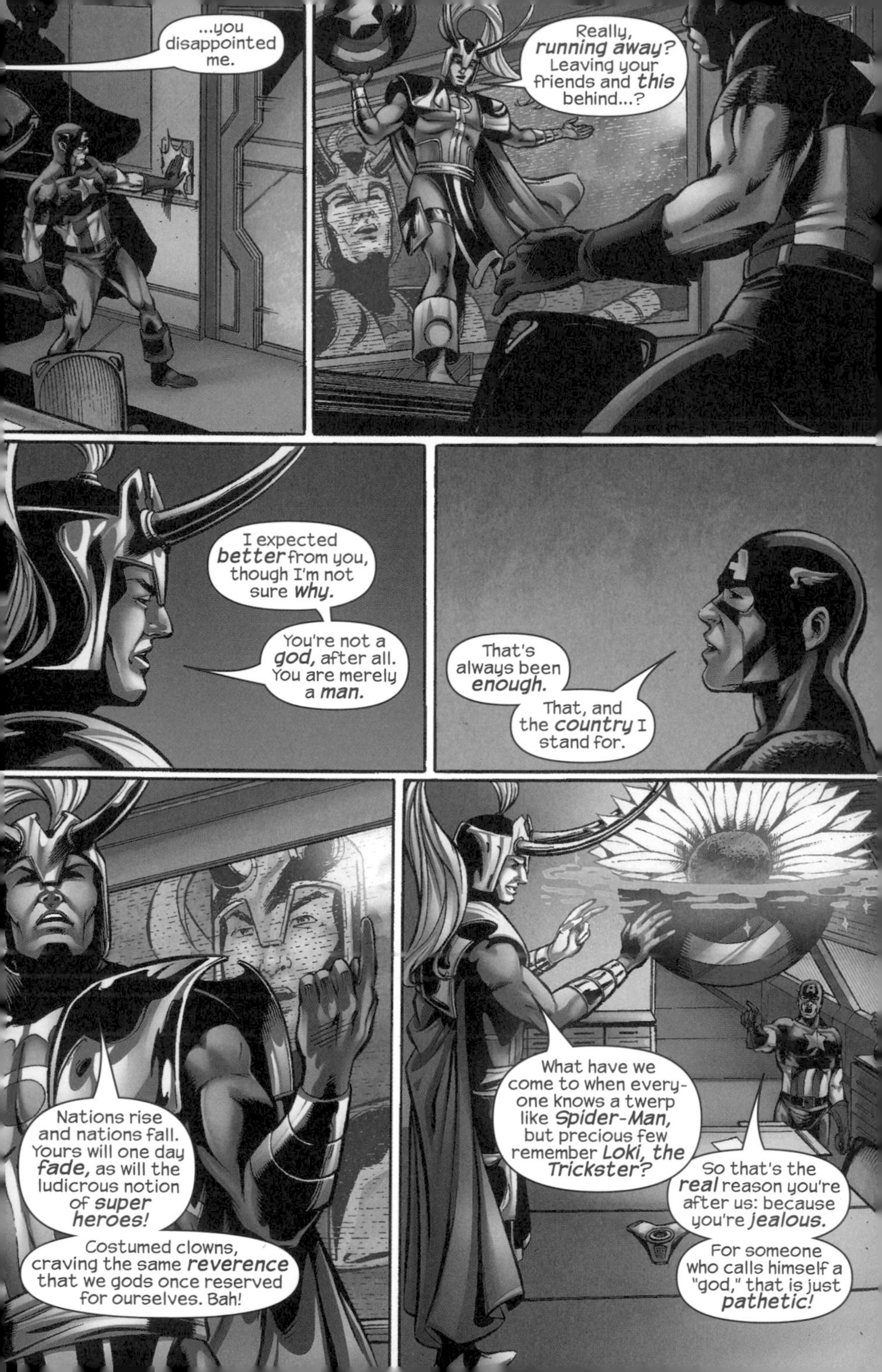

...you disappointed me.
Really, *running away?* Leaving your friends and *this* behind...?
I expected *better* from you, though I'm not sure *why.*
You're not a *god,* after all. You are merely a *man.*
That's always been *enough.*
That, and the *country* I stand for.
Nations rise and nations fall. Yours will one day *fade,* as will the ludicrous notion of *super heroes!*
Costumed clowns, craving the same *reverence* that we gods once reserved for ourselves. Bah!
What have we come to when every-one knows a twerp like *Spider-Man,* but precious few remember *Loki, the Trickster?*
So that's the *real* reason you're after us: because you're *jealous.*
For someone who calls himself a "god," that is just *pathetic!*

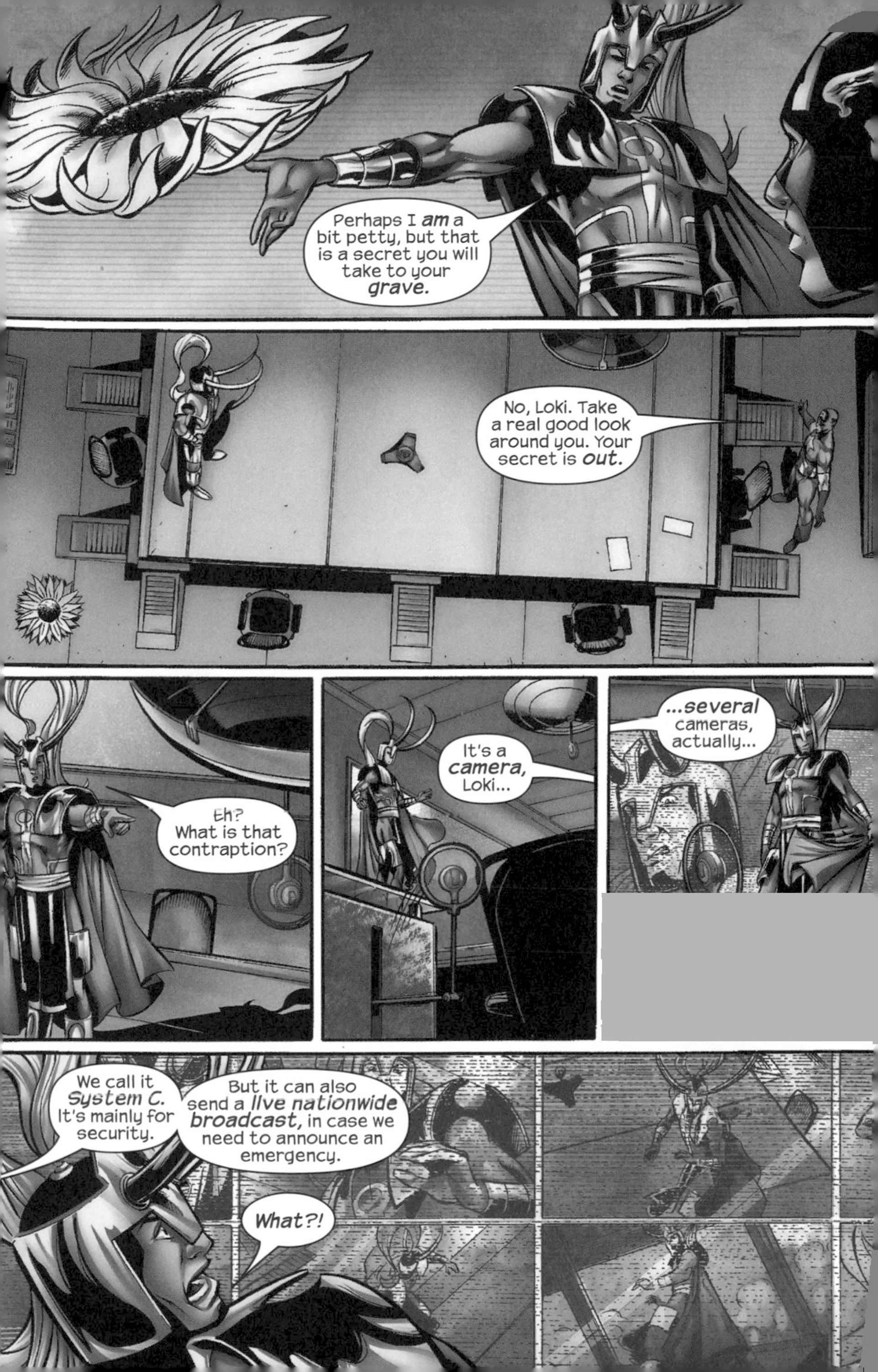
Perhaps I *am* a bit petty, but that is a secret you will take to your *grave.*
No, Loki. Take a real good look around you. Your secret is *out.*
Eh? What is that contraption?
It's a *camera,* Loki...
...*several* cameras, actually...
We call it *System C.* It's mainly for security.
But it can also send a *live nationwide broadcast,* in case we need to announce an emergency.
What?!

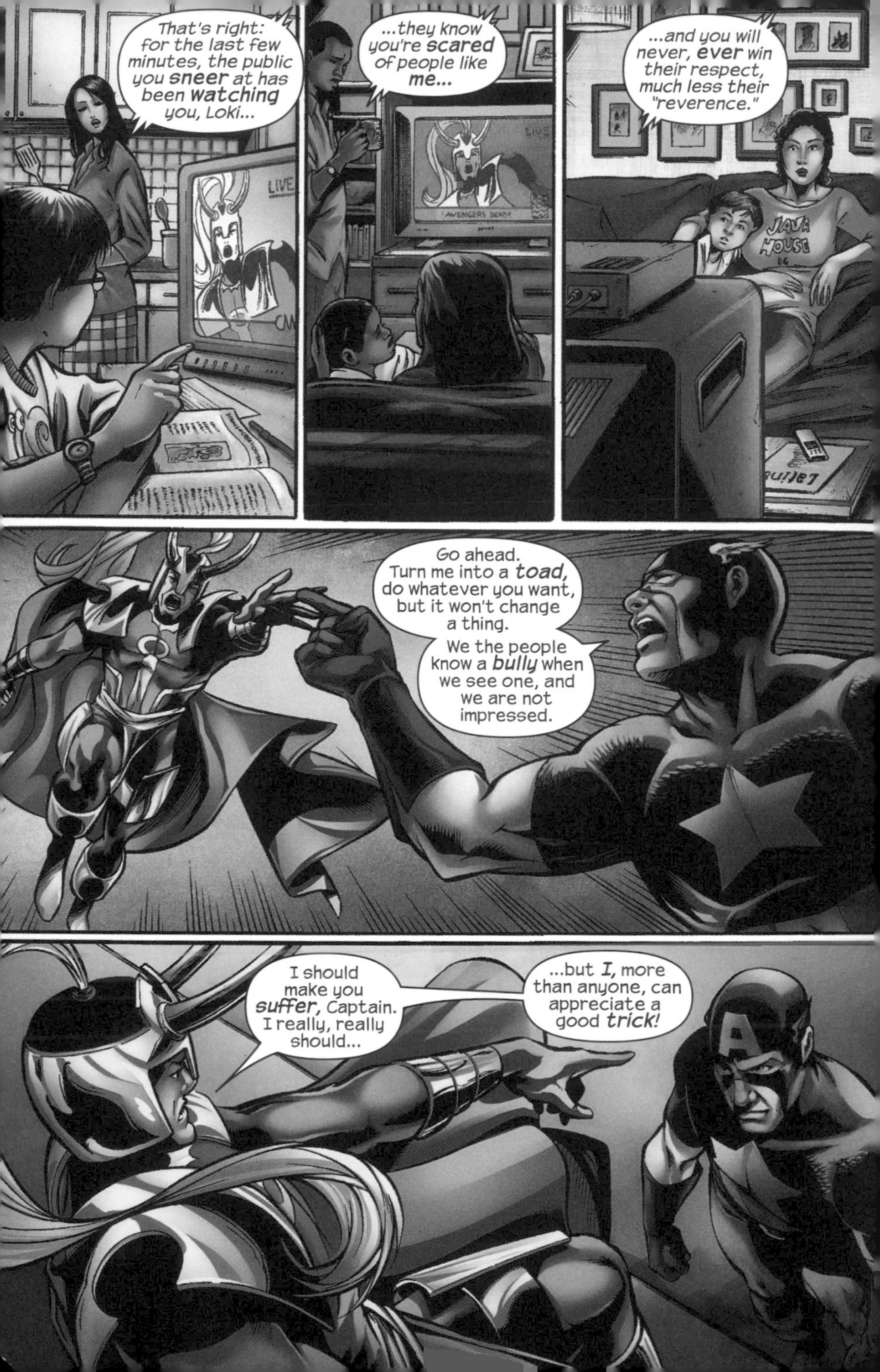
That's right: for the last few minutes, the public you sneer at has been watching you, Loki...
LIVE
...they know you're scared of people like me...
AVENGERS DEAD?
...and you will never, ever win their respect, much less their "reverence."
JAVA HOUSE
Go ahead. Turn me into a toad, do whatever you want, but it won't change a thing.
We the people know a bully when we see one, and we are not impressed.
I should make you suffer, Captain. I really, really should...
...but I, more than anyone, can appreciate a good trick!

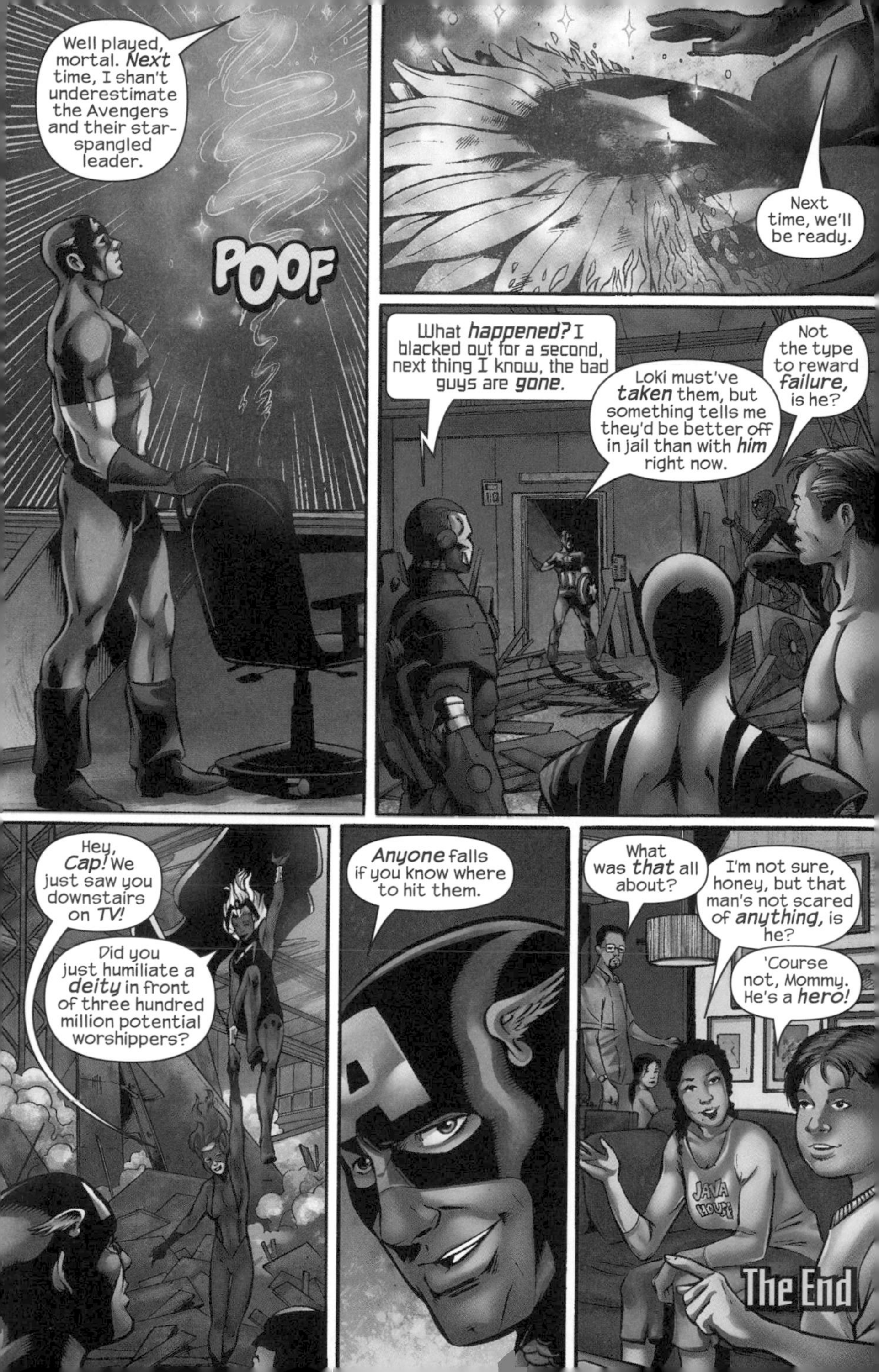

Well played, mortal. Next time, I shan't underestimate the Avengers and their star-spangled leader.
POOF
Next time, we'll be ready.
What happened? I blacked out for a second, next thing I know, the bad guys are gone.
Loki must've taken them, but something tells me they'd be better off in jail than with him right now.
Not the type to reward failure, is he?
Hey, Cap! We just saw you downstairs on TV!
Did you just humiliate a deity in front of three hundred million potential worshippers?
Anyone falls if you know where to hit them.
What was that all about?
I'm not sure, honey, but that man's not scared of anything, is he?
'Course not, Mommy. He's a hero!
JAVA HOUSE
The End

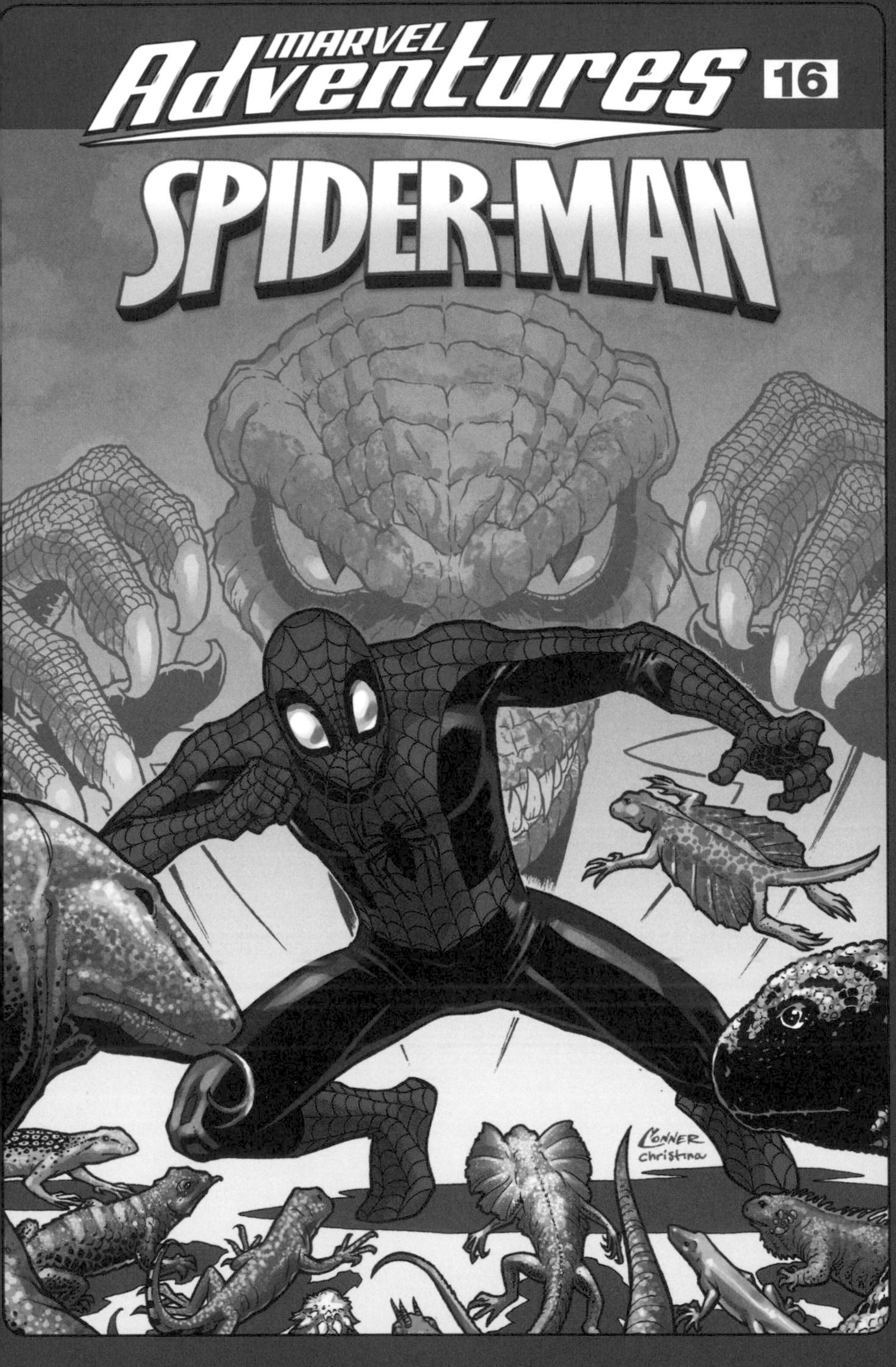
MARVEL
Adventures
16
SPIDER-MAN
CONNER
christina

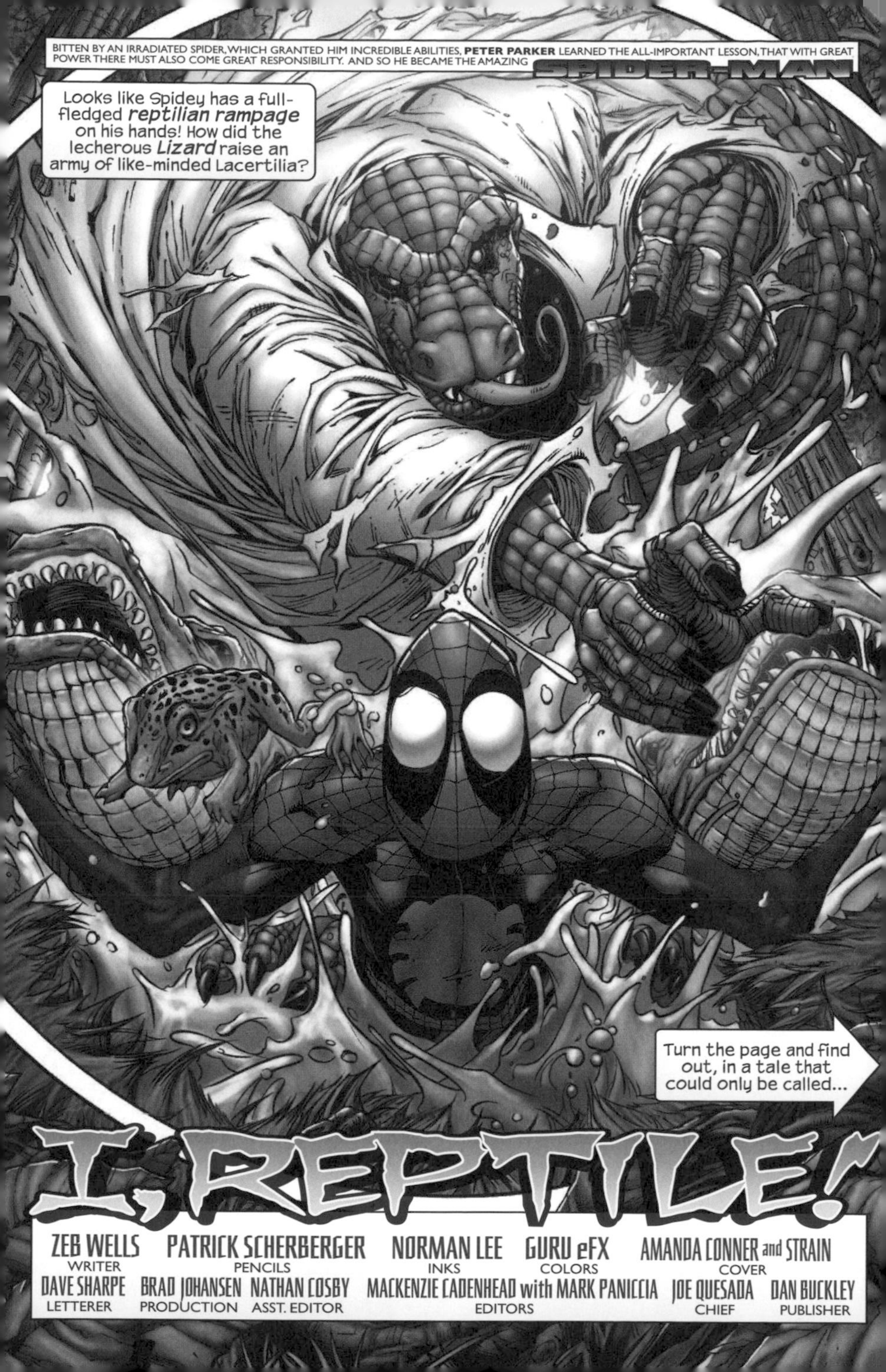

BITTEN BY AN IRRADIATED SPIDER, WHICH GRANTED HIM INCREDIBLE ABILITIES, PETER PARKER LEARNED THE ALL-IMPORTANT LESSON, THAT WITH GREAT POWER THERE MUST ALSO COME GREAT RESPONSIBILITY. AND SO HE BECAME THE AMAZING
SPIDER-MAN
Looks like Spidey has a full-fledged reptilian rampage on his hands! How did the lecherous Lizard raise an army of like-minded Lacertilia?
Turn the page and find out, in a tale that could only be called...
I, REPTILE!
ZEB WELLS WRITER
PATRICK SCHERBERGER PENCILS
NORMAN LEE INKS
GURU eFX COLORS
AMANDA CONNER and STRAIN COVER
DAVE SHARPE LETTERER
BRAD JOHANSEN PRODUCTION
NATHAN COSBY ASST. EDITOR
MACKENZIE CADENHEAD with MARK PANICCIA EDITORS
JOE QUESADA CHIEF
DAN BUCKLEY PUBLISHER

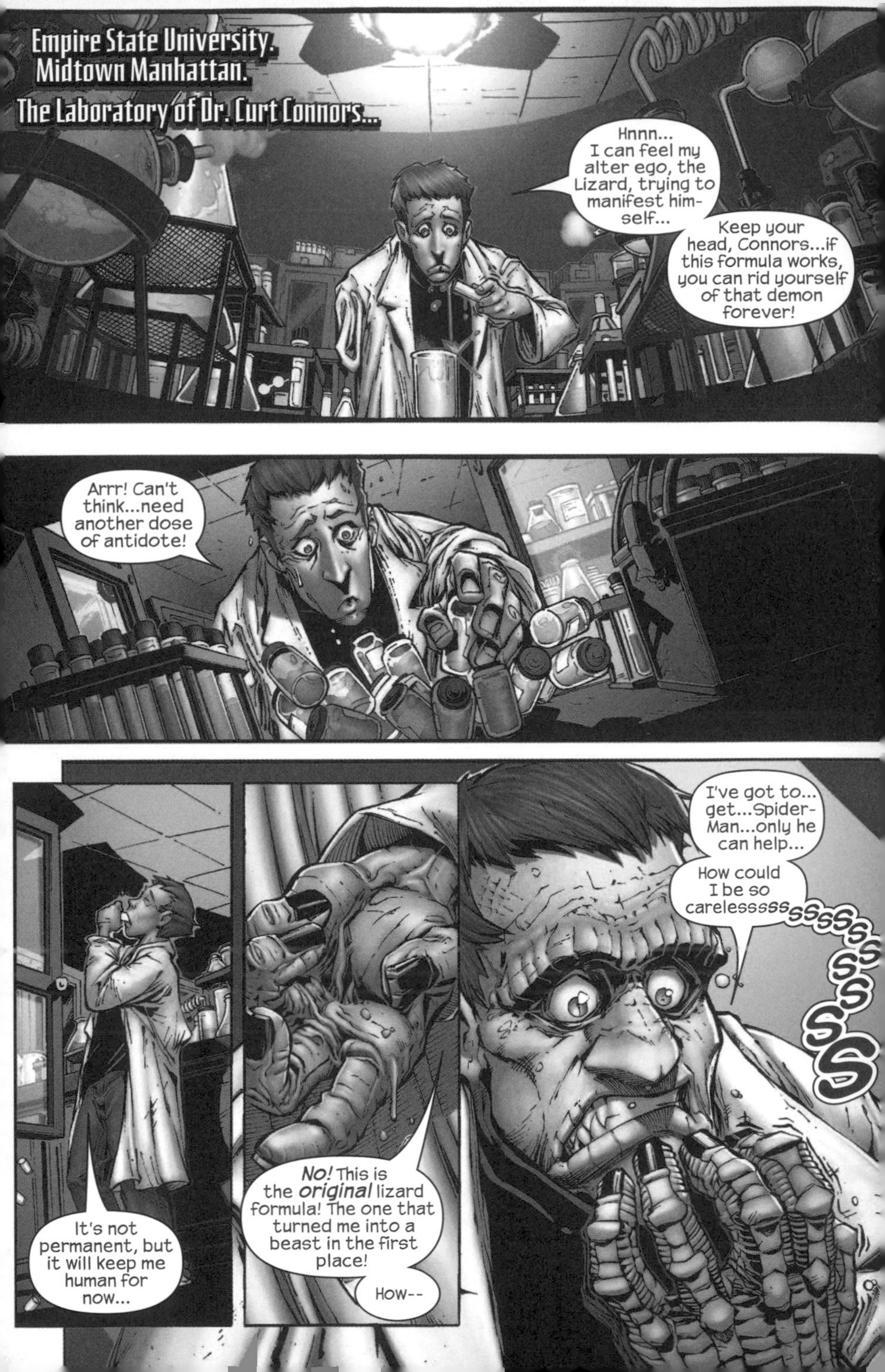
Empire State University.
Midtown Manhattan.
The Laboratory of Dr. Curt Connors...
Hnnn... I can feel my alter ego, the Lizard, trying to manifest him-self...
Keep your head, Connors...if this formula works, you can rid yourself of that demon forever!
Arrr! Can't think...need another dose of antidote!
It's not permanent, but it will keep me human for now...
No! This is the original lizard formula! The one that turned me into a beast in the first place!
How--
I've got to... get...Spider-Man...only he can help...
How could I be so carelesssssSSSSSSSSSSS

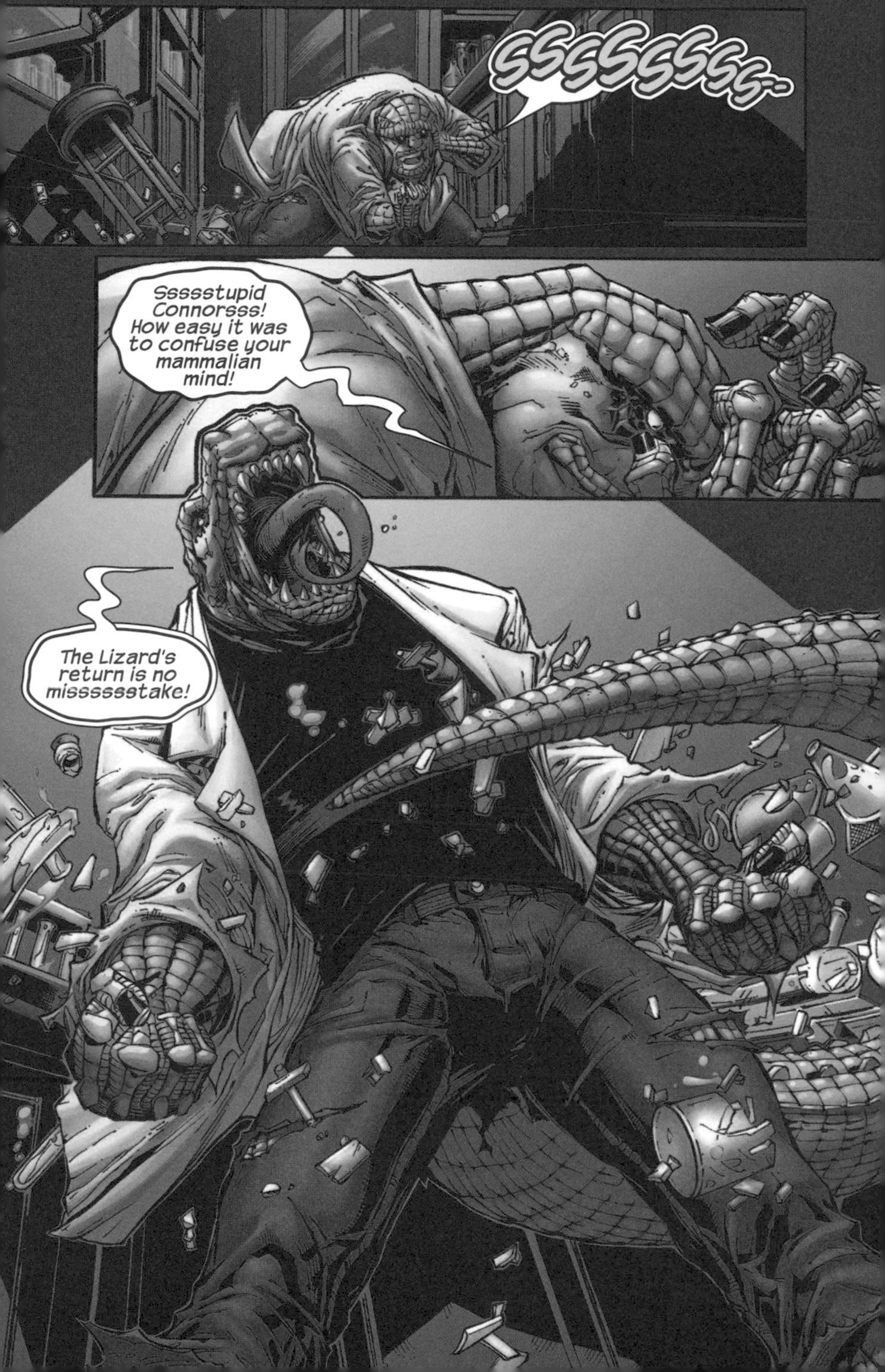
SSSSSSSSS-
Sssssstupid Connorsss! How easy it was to confuse your mammalian mind!
The Lizard's return is no missssssstake!

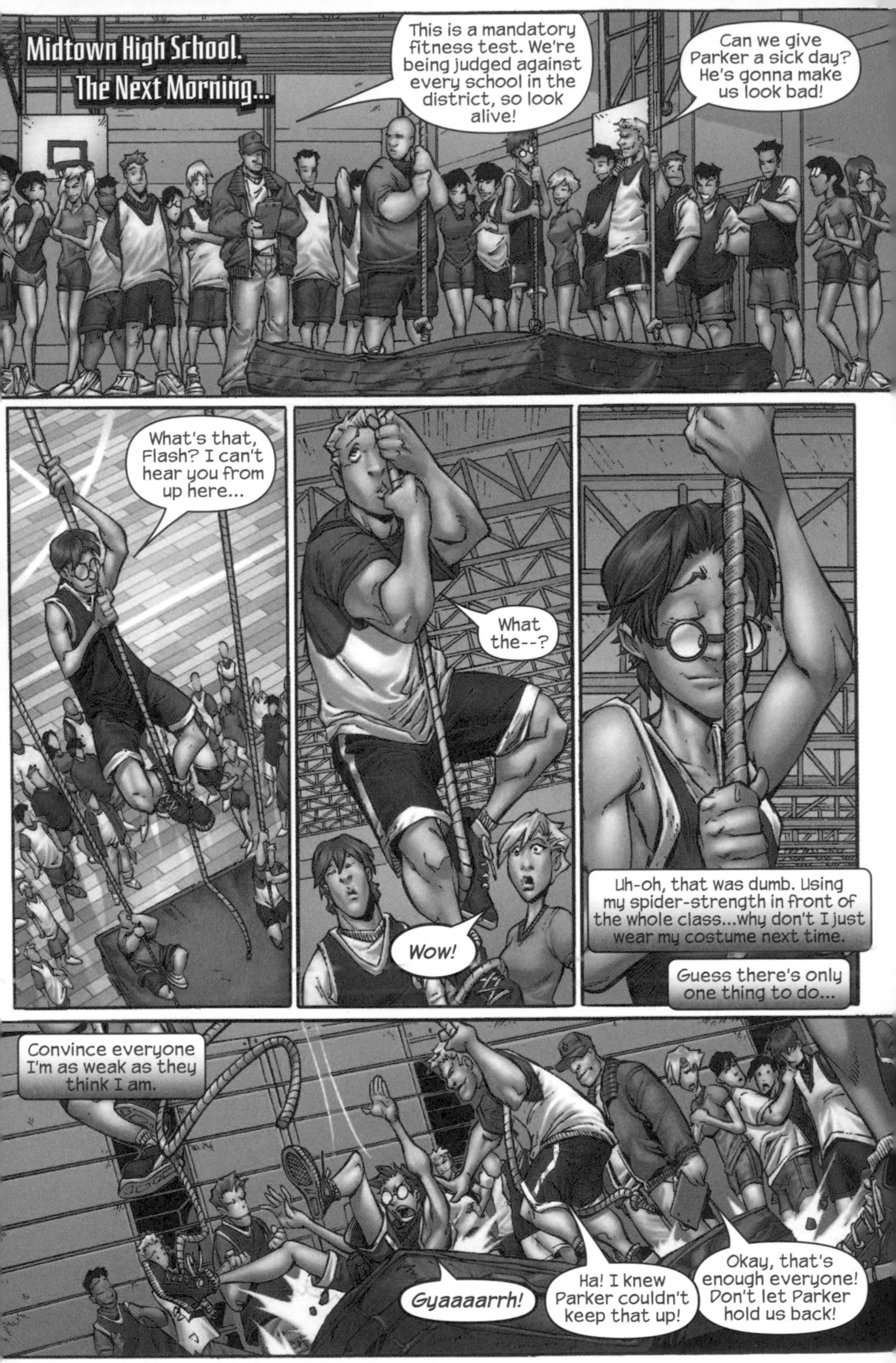
Midtown High School.
The Next Morning...
This is a mandatory fitness test. We're being judged against every school in the district, so look alive!
Can we give Parker a sick day? He's gonna make us look bad!
What's that, Flash? I can't hear you from up here...
What the--?
Wow!
Uh-oh, that was dumb. Using my spider-strength in front of the whole class...why don't I just wear my costume next time.
Guess there's only one thing to do...
Convince everyone I'm as weak as they think I am.
Gyaaaarrh!
Ha! I knew Parker couldn't keep that up!
Okay, that's enough everyone! Don't let Parker hold us back!

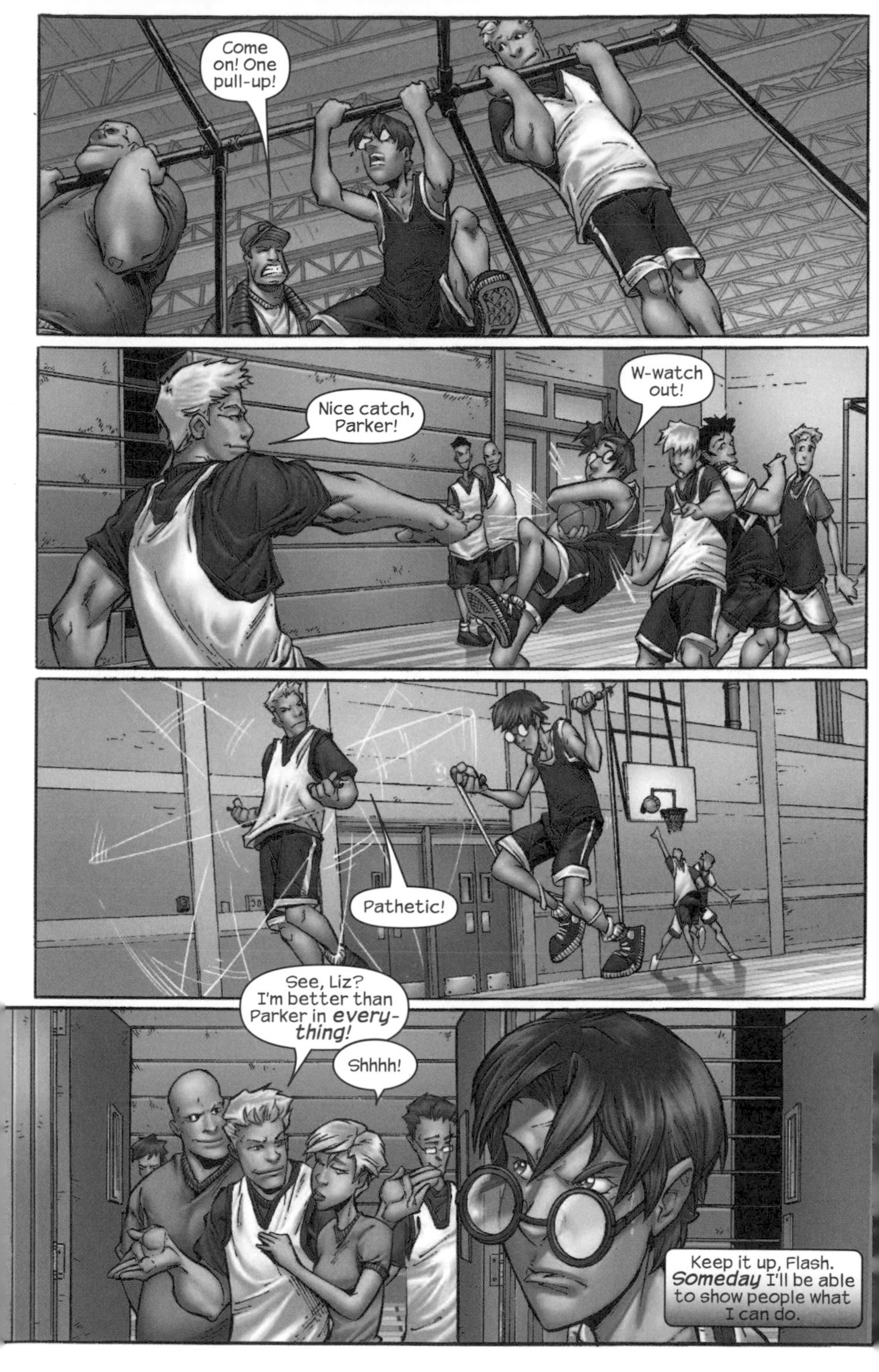
Come on! One pull-up!
Nice catch, Parker!
W-watch out!
Pathetic!
See, Liz? I'm better than Parker in *every-thing!*
Shhhh!
Keep it up, Flash. *Someday* I'll be able to show people what I can do.

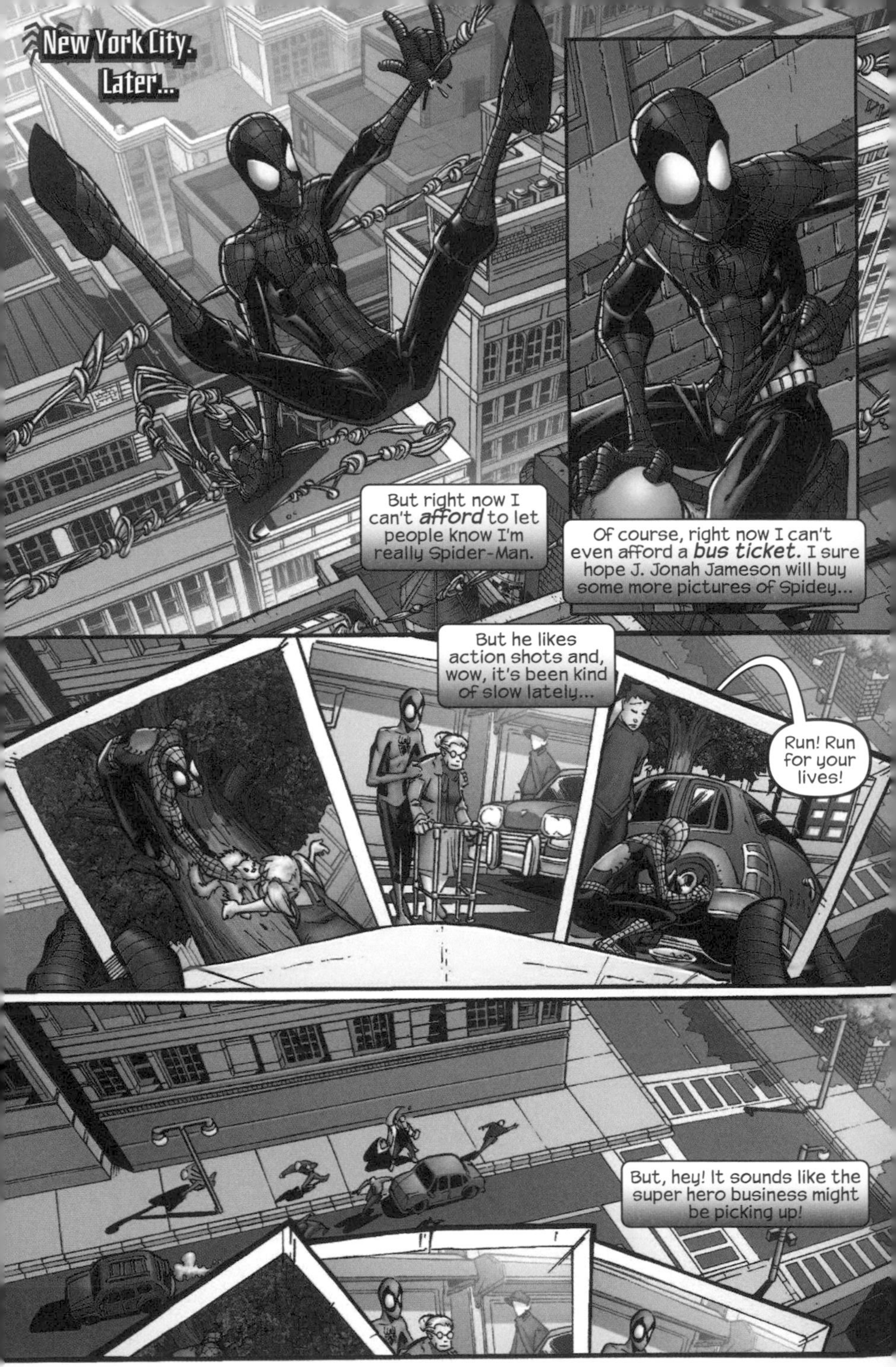
New York City. Later...
But right now I can't *afford* to let people know I'm really Spider-Man.
Of course, right now I can't even afford a *bus ticket.* I sure hope J. Jonah Jameson will buy some more pictures of Spidey...
But he likes action shots and, wow, it's been kind of slow lately...
Run! Run for your lives!
But, hey! It sounds like the super hero business might be picking up!

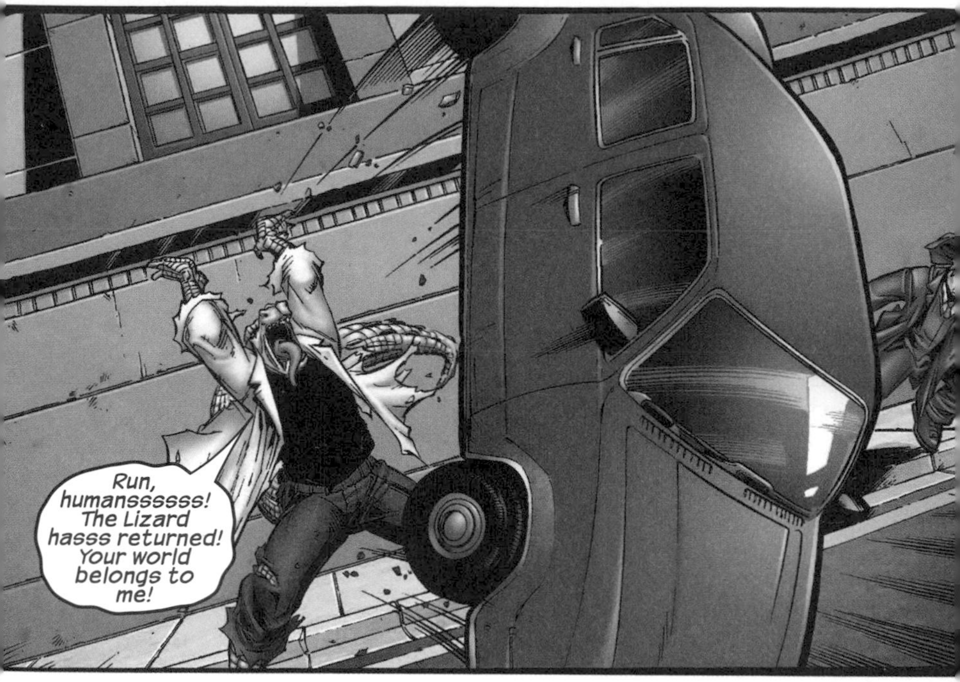
Run, humanssssss! The Lizard hasss returned! Your world belongs to me!

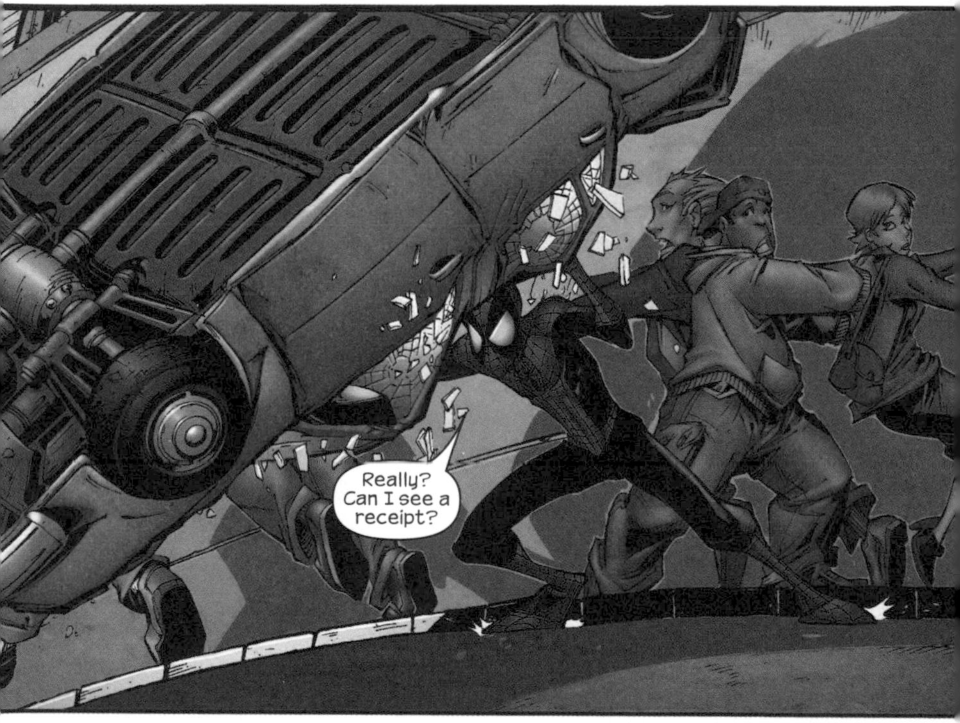
Really? Can I see a receipt?

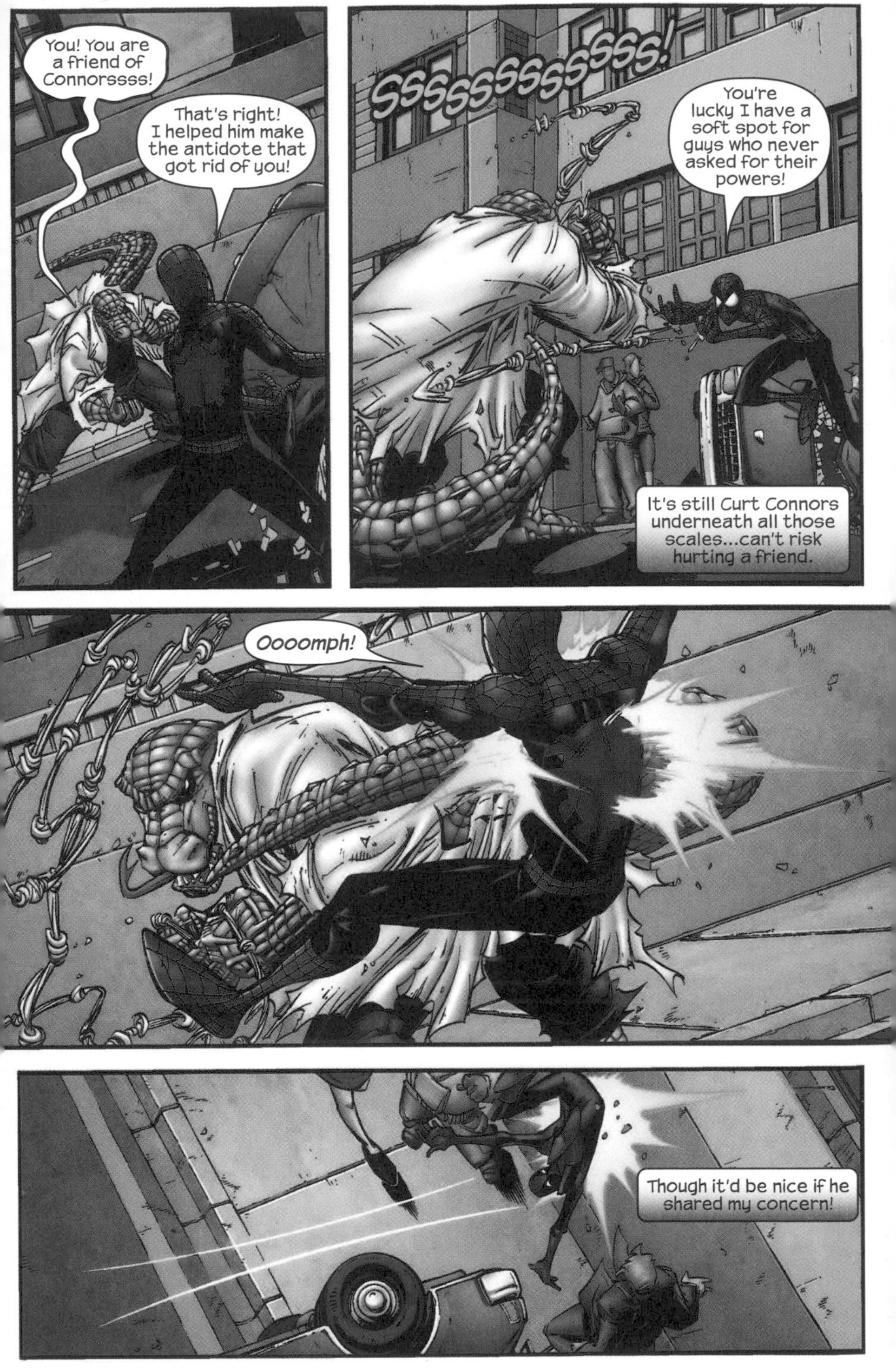
You! You are a friend of Connorssss!
That's right! I helped him make the antidote that got rid of you!
SSSSSSSSSSSSSS!
You're lucky I have a soft spot for guys who never asked for their powers!
It's still Curt Connors underneath all those scales...can't risk hurting a friend.
Oooomph!
Though it'd be nice if he shared my concern!

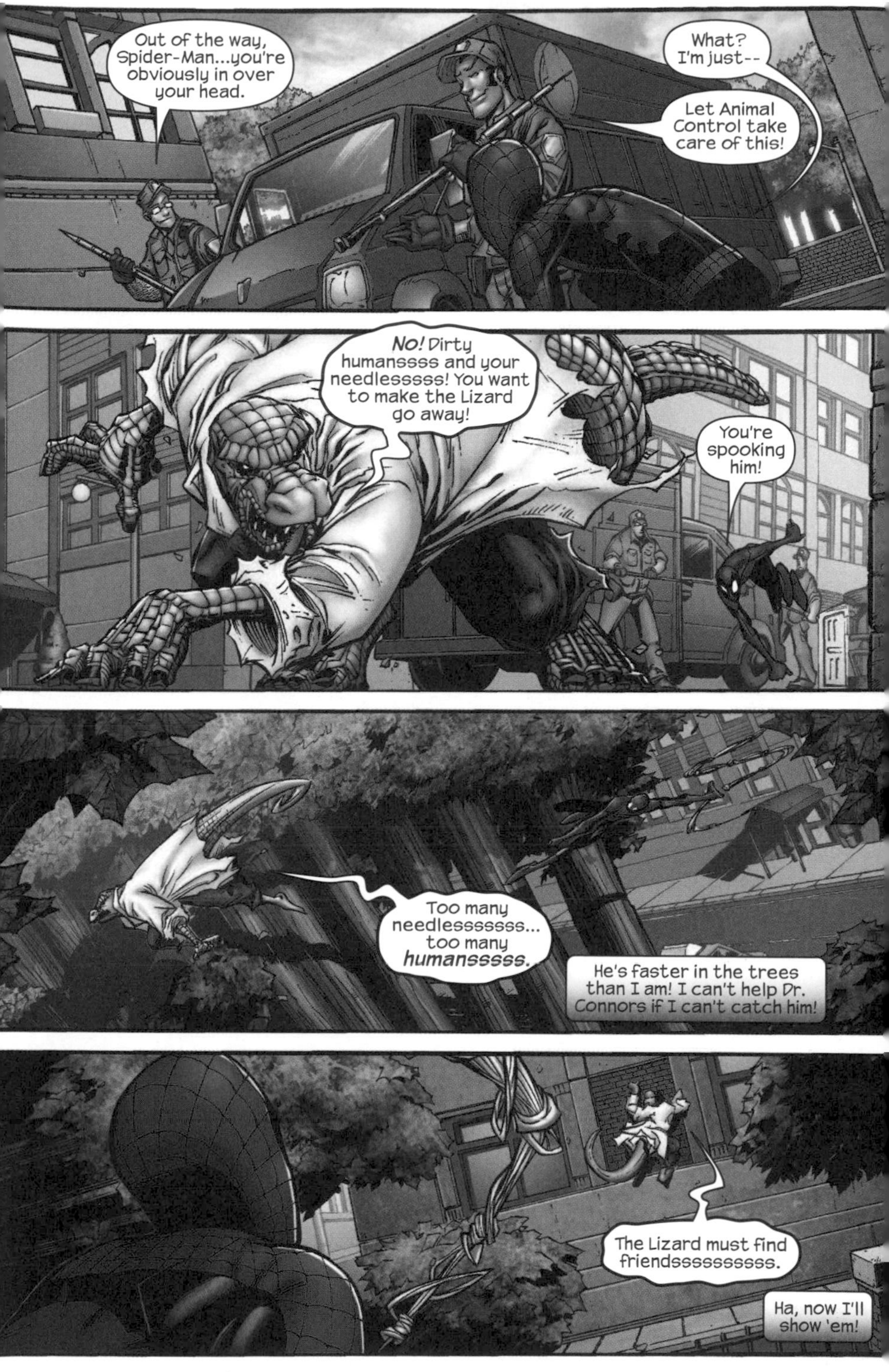

Out of the way, Spider-Man...you're obviously in over your head.
What? I'm just--
Let Animal Control take care of this!
No! Dirty humanssss and your needlesssss! You want to make the Lizard go away!
You're spooking him!
Too many needlessssss... too many humanssss.
He's faster in the trees than I am! I can't help Dr. Connors if I can't catch him!
The Lizard must find friendsssssssss.
Ha, now I'll show 'em!

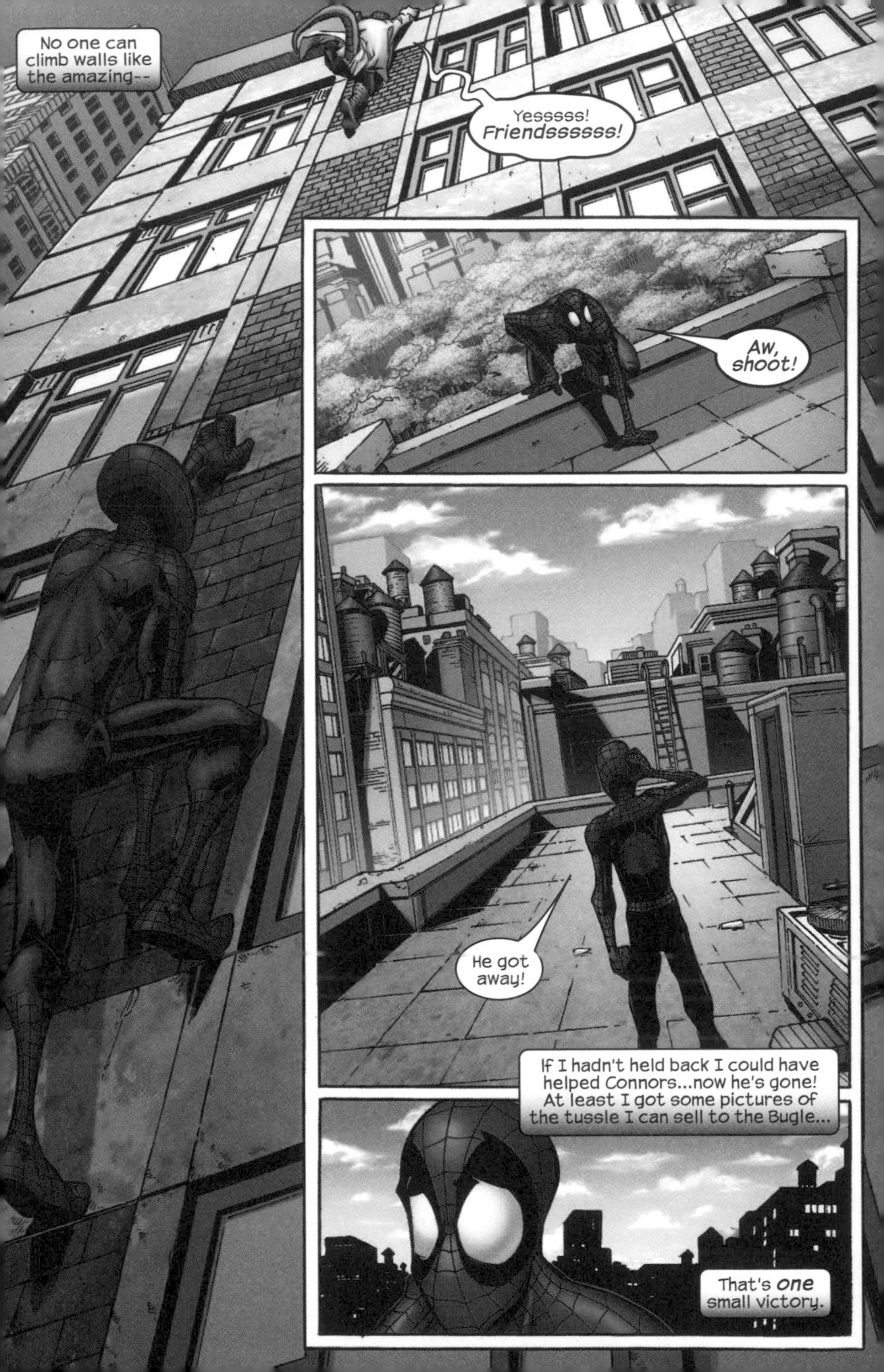
No one can climb walls like the amazing--
Yesssss! Friendssssss!
Aw, shoot!
He got away!
If I hadn't held back I could have helped Connors...now he's gone! At least I got some pictures of the tussle I can sell to the Bugle...
That's one small victory.

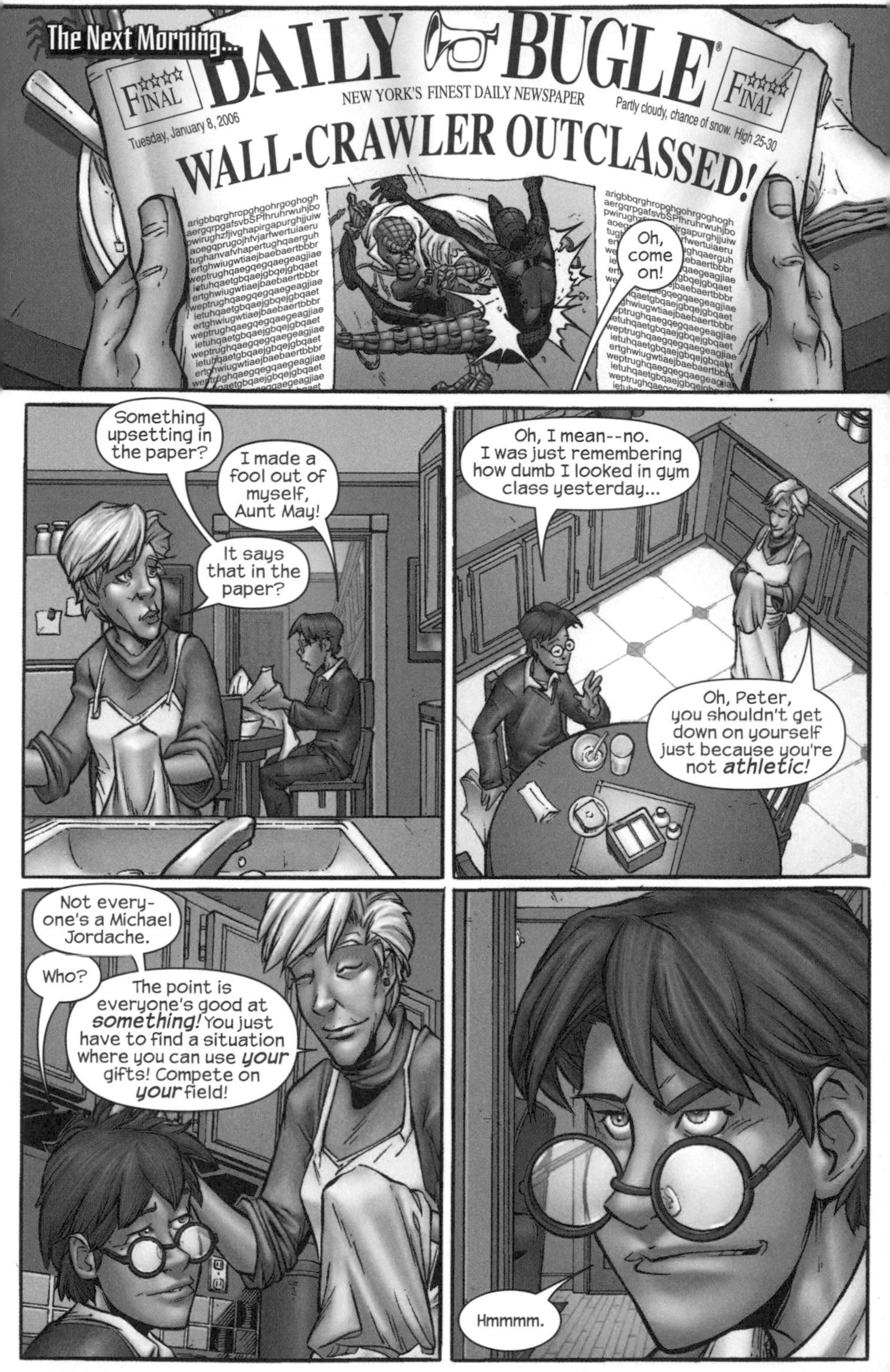

The Next Morning...
DAILY BUGLE
FINAL
NEW YORK'S FINEST DAILY NEWSPAPER
Tuesday, January 8, 2006
Partly cloudy, chance of snow. High 25-30
WALL-CRAWLER OUTCLASSED!
Oh, come on!
Something upsetting in the paper?
I made a fool out of myself, Aunt May!
It says that in the paper?
Oh, I mean--no. I was just remembering how dumb I looked in gym class yesterday...
Oh, Peter, you shouldn't get down on yourself just because you're not *athletic!*
Not every-one's a Michael Jordache.
Who?
The point is everyone's good at *something!* You just have to find a situation where you can use *your* gifts! Compete on *your* field!
Hmmmm.

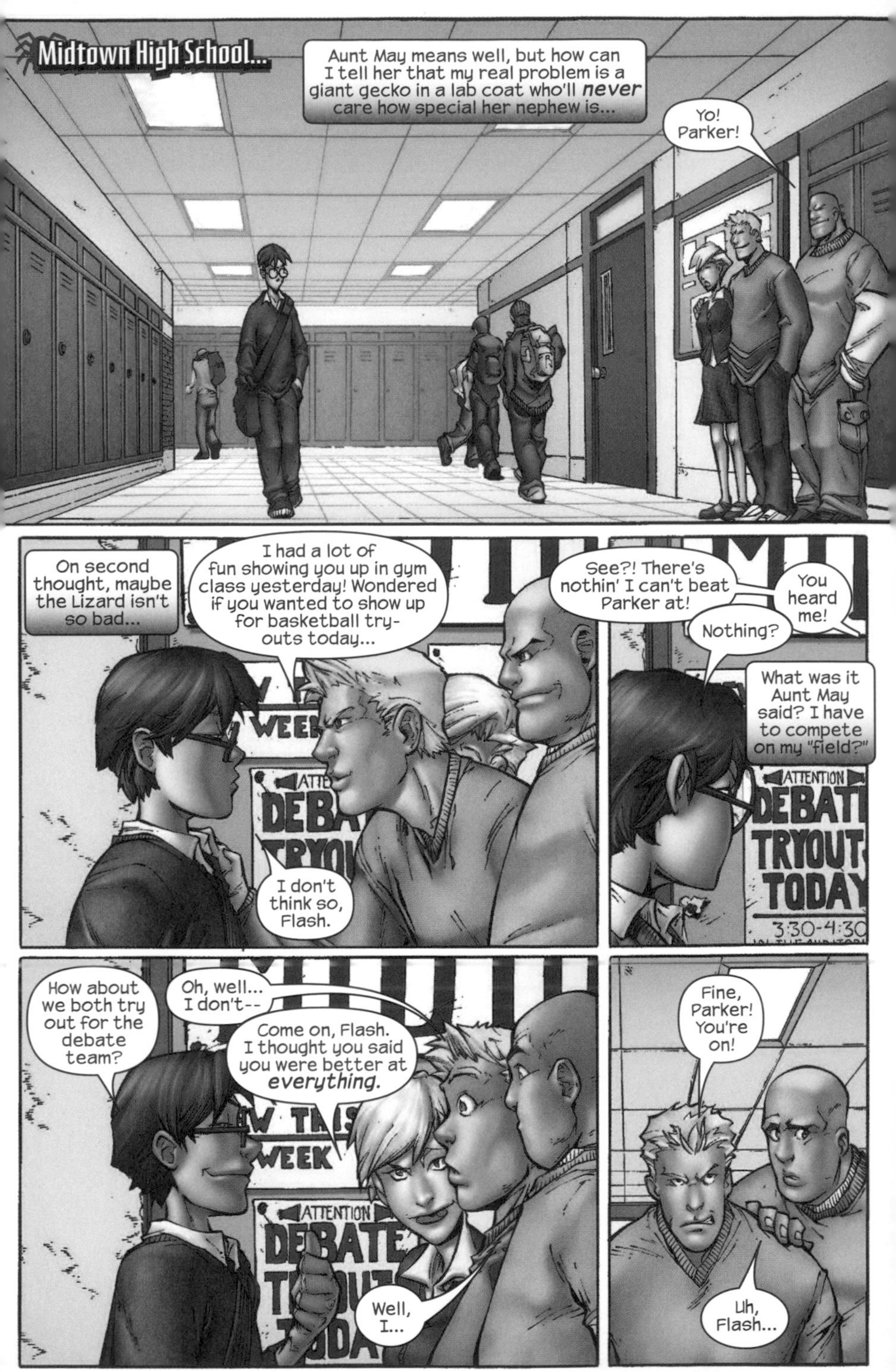

Midtown High School...
Aunt May means well, but how can I tell her that my real problem is a giant gecko in a lab coat who'll *never* care how special her nephew is...
Yo! Parker!
On second thought, maybe the Lizard isn't so bad...
I had a lot of fun showing you up in gym class yesterday! Wondered if you wanted to show up for basketball try-outs today...
I don't think so, Flash.
See?! There's nothin' I can't beat Parker at!
You heard me!
Nothing?
What was it Aunt May said? I have to compete on my "field?"
ATTENTION
DEBATE TRYOUTS TODAY
3:30-4:30
How about we both try out for the debate team?
Oh, well... I don't--
Come on, Flash. I thought you said you were better at *everything.*
Well, I...
Fine, Parker! You're on!
Uh, Flash...

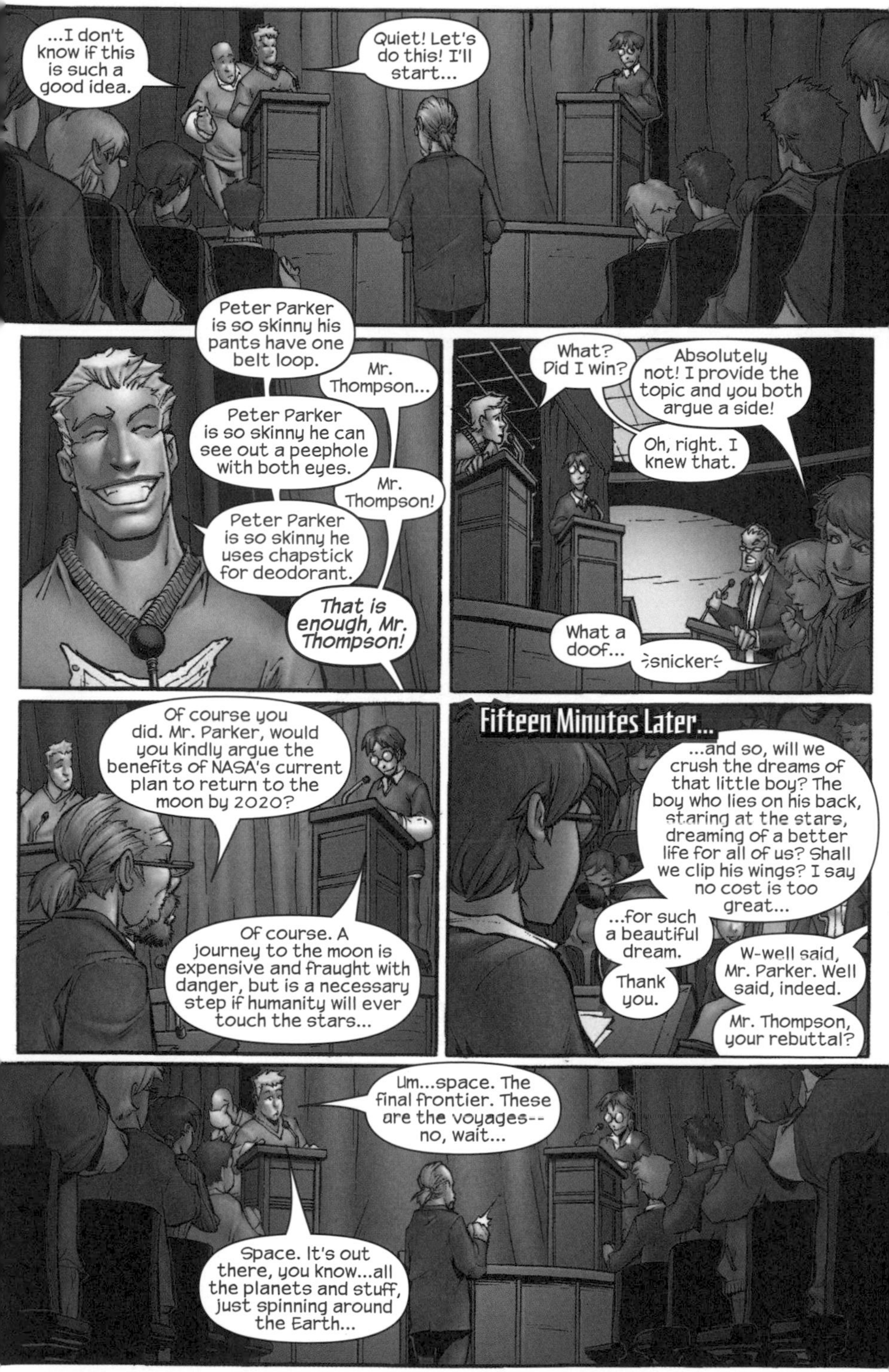
...I don't know if this is such a good idea.
Quiet! Let's do this! I'll start...
Peter Parker is so skinny his pants have one belt loop.
Mr. Thompson...
Peter Parker is so skinny he can see out a peephole with both eyes.
Mr. Thompson!
Peter Parker is so skinny he uses chapstick for deodorant.
That is enough, Mr. Thompson!
What? Did I win?
Absolutely not! I provide the topic and you both argue a side!
Oh, right. I knew that.
What a doof...
snicker
Of course you did. Mr. Parker, would you kindly argue the benefits of NASA's current plan to return to the moon by 2020?
Of course. A journey to the moon is expensive and fraught with danger, but is a necessary step if humanity will ever touch the stars...
Fifteen Minutes Later...
...and so, will we crush the dreams of that little boy? The boy who lies on his back, staring at the stars, dreaming of a better life for all of us? Shall we clip his wings? I say no cost is too great...
...for such a beautiful dream.
Thank you.
W-well said, Mr. Parker. Well said, indeed.
Mr. Thompson, your rebuttal?
Um...space. The final frontier. These are the voyages--no, wait...
Space. It's out there, you know...all the planets and stuff, just spinning around the Earth...

Later...

Peter! Peter, wait up!

Peter, that was *amazing.*

Oh, thanks, Liz.

So...what are you doing Saturday night?

Oh, well I--

EEEEEEEEEEEEE!

Getitoff getitoff getitoff!

Liz, try and relax.

They're not attacking... they all seem to be heading somewhere as a group.

B-but where?

Peter?

Sorry to run, Liz...

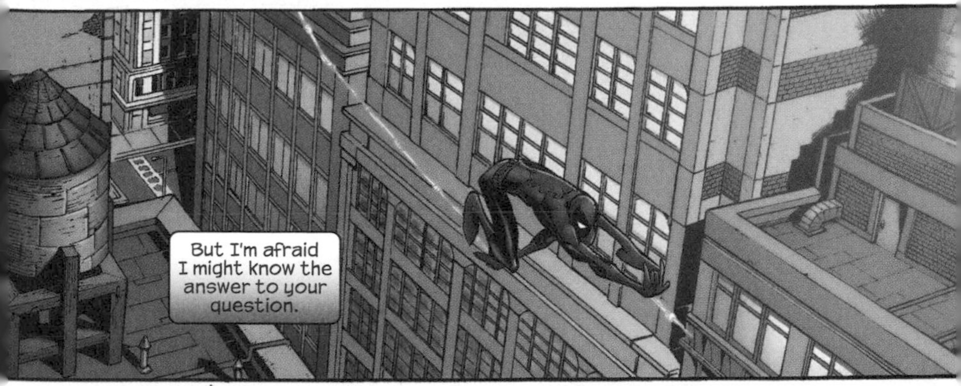
But I'm afraid I might know the answer to your question.

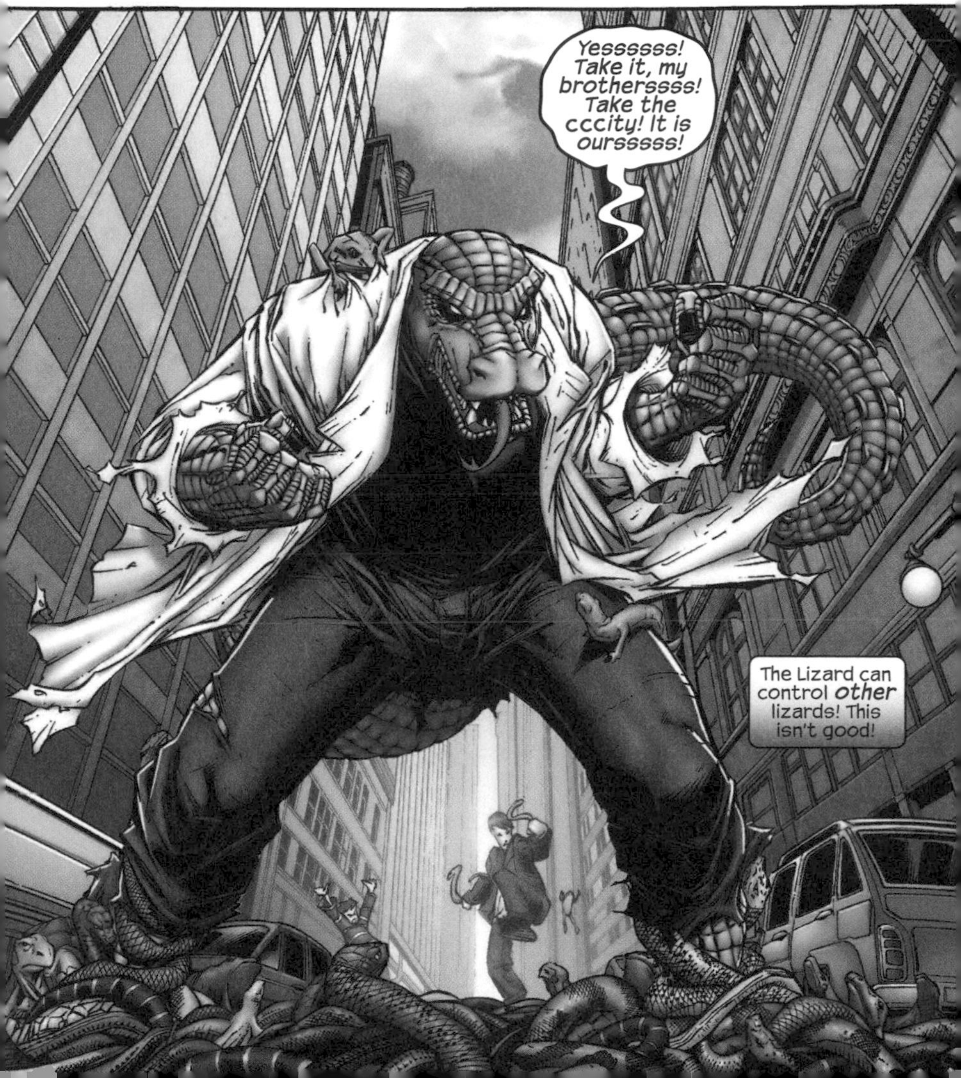
Yessssss! Take it, my brotherssss! Take the cccity! It is oursssss!
The Lizard can control *other* lizards! This isn't good!

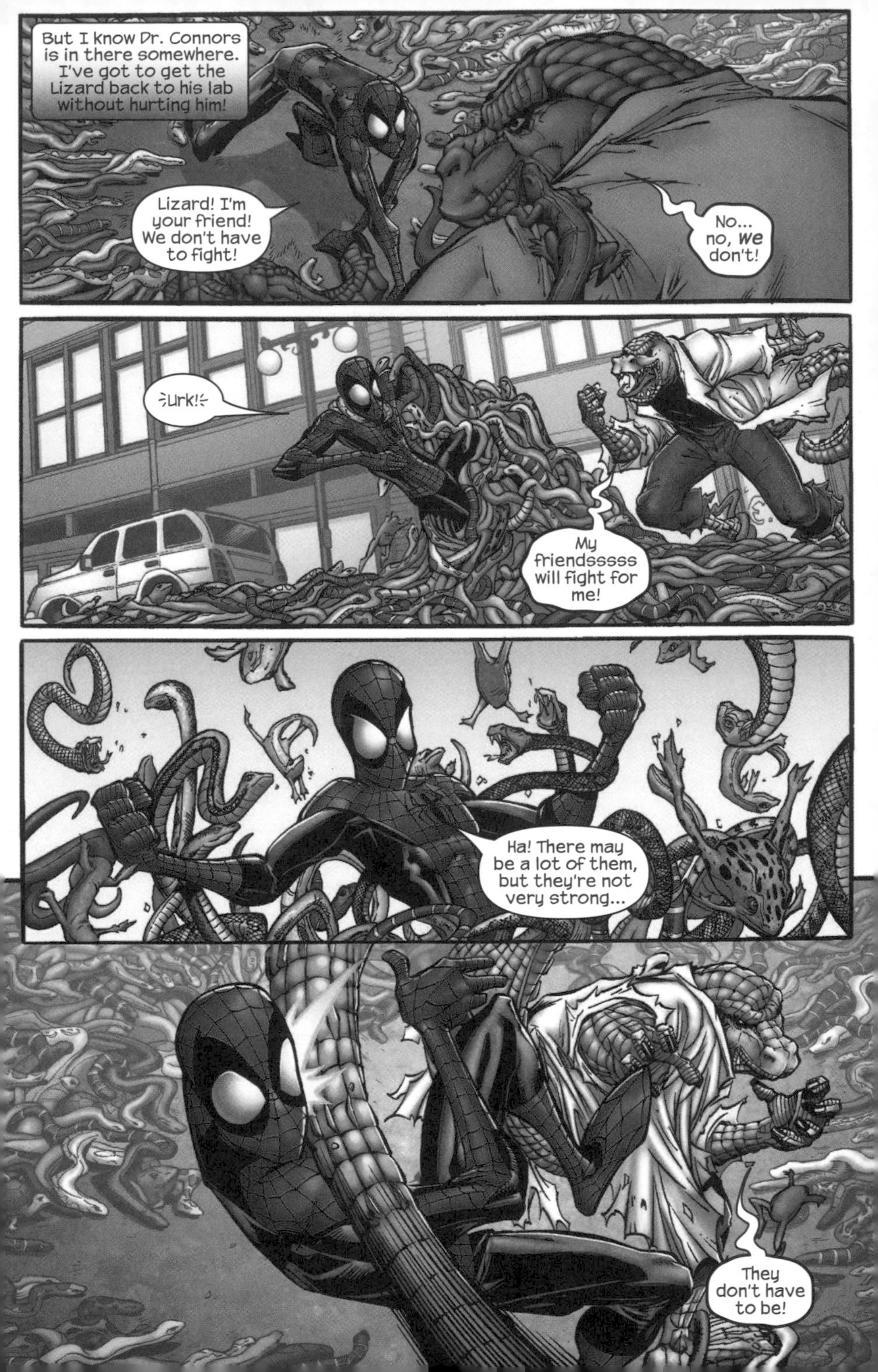
But I know Dr. Connors is in there somewhere. I've got to get the Lizard back to his lab without hurting him!
Lizard! I'm your friend! We don't have to fight!
No... no, **we** don't!
Urk!
My friendsssss will fight for me!
Ha! There may be a lot of them, but they're not very strong...
They don't have to be!

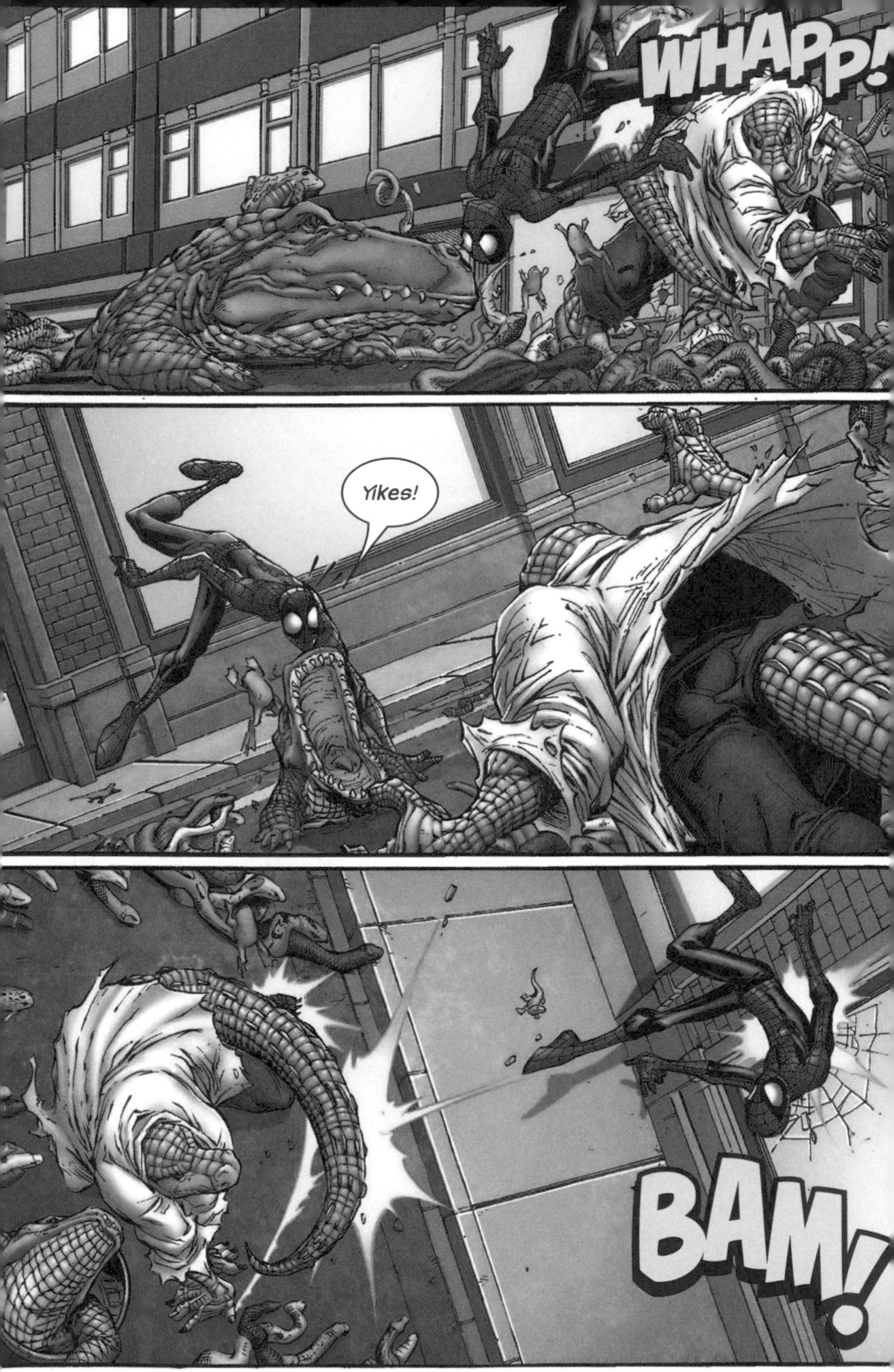
WHAPP!
Yikes!
BAM!

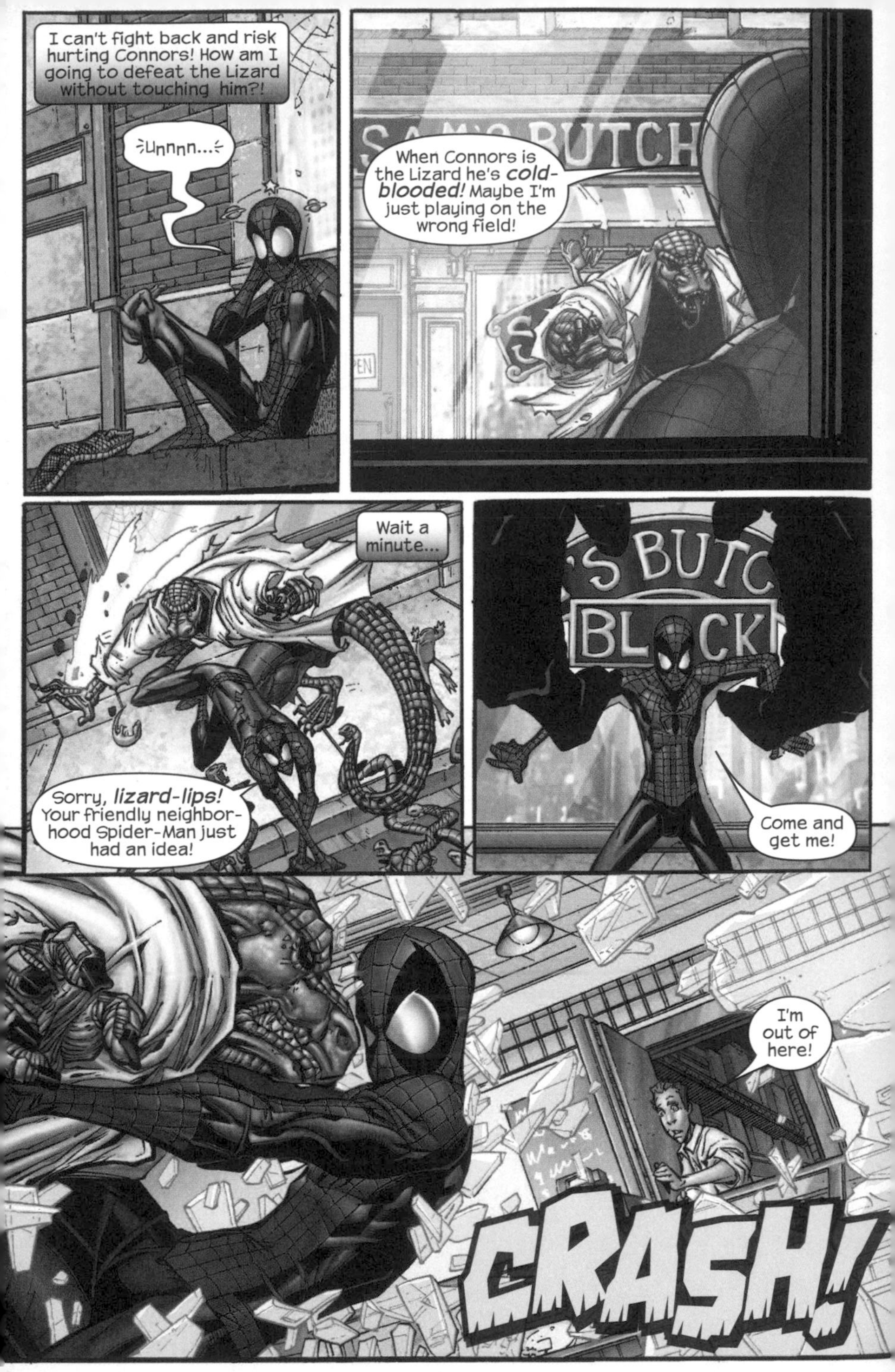
I can't fight back and risk hurting Connors! How am I going to defeat the Lizard without touching him?!
Unnnn...
When Connors is the Lizard he's *cold-blooded!* Maybe I'm just playing on the wrong field!
SAM'S BUTCH
Wait a minute...
Sorry, *lizard-lips!* Your friendly neighbor-hood Spider-Man just had an idea!
'S BUTC
BL CK
Come and get me!
I'm out of here!
CRASH!

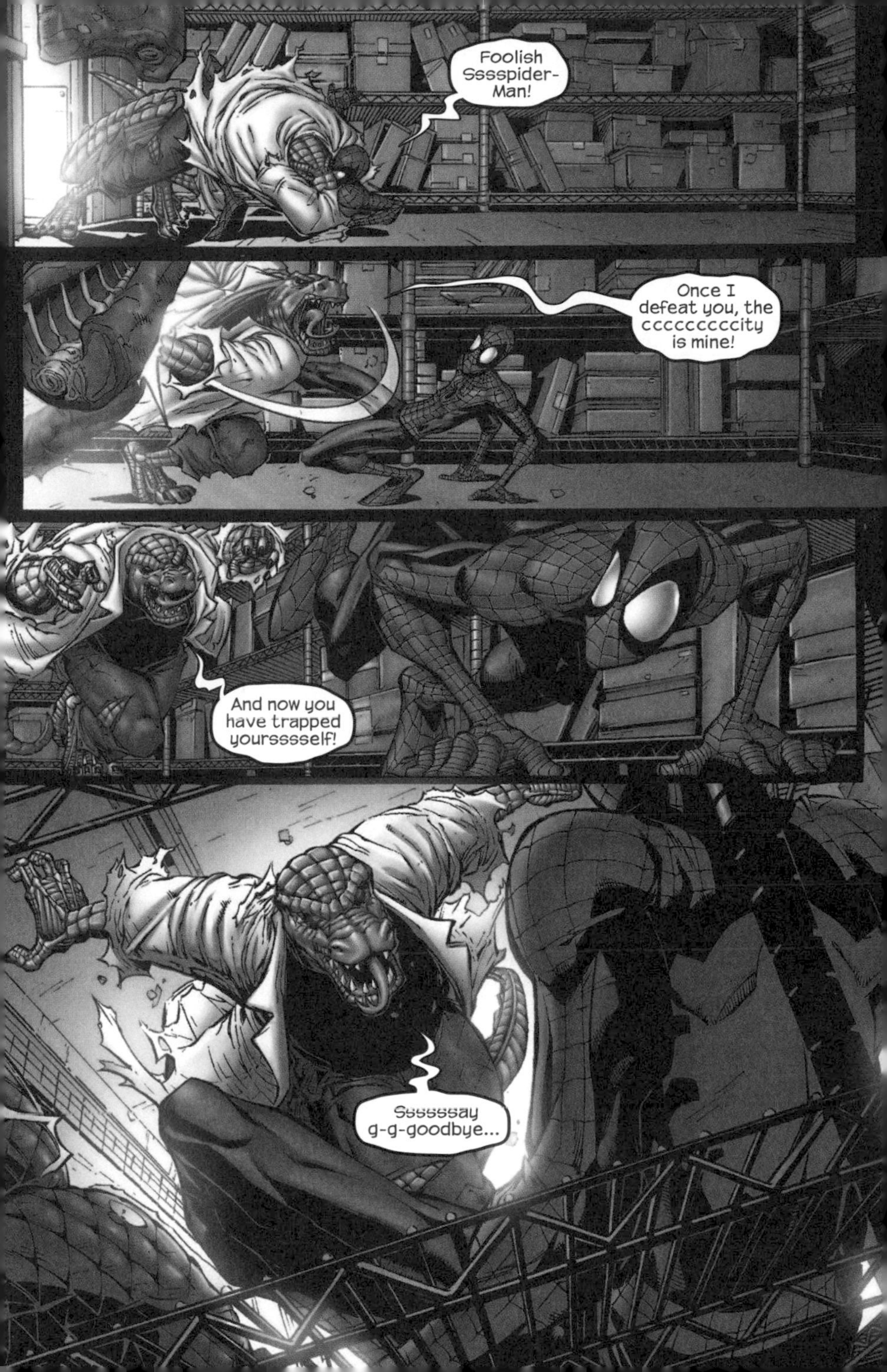
Foolish Sssspider-Man!
Once I defeat you, the cccccccccity is mine!
And now you have trapped yourssssself!
Sssssssay g-g-goodbye...

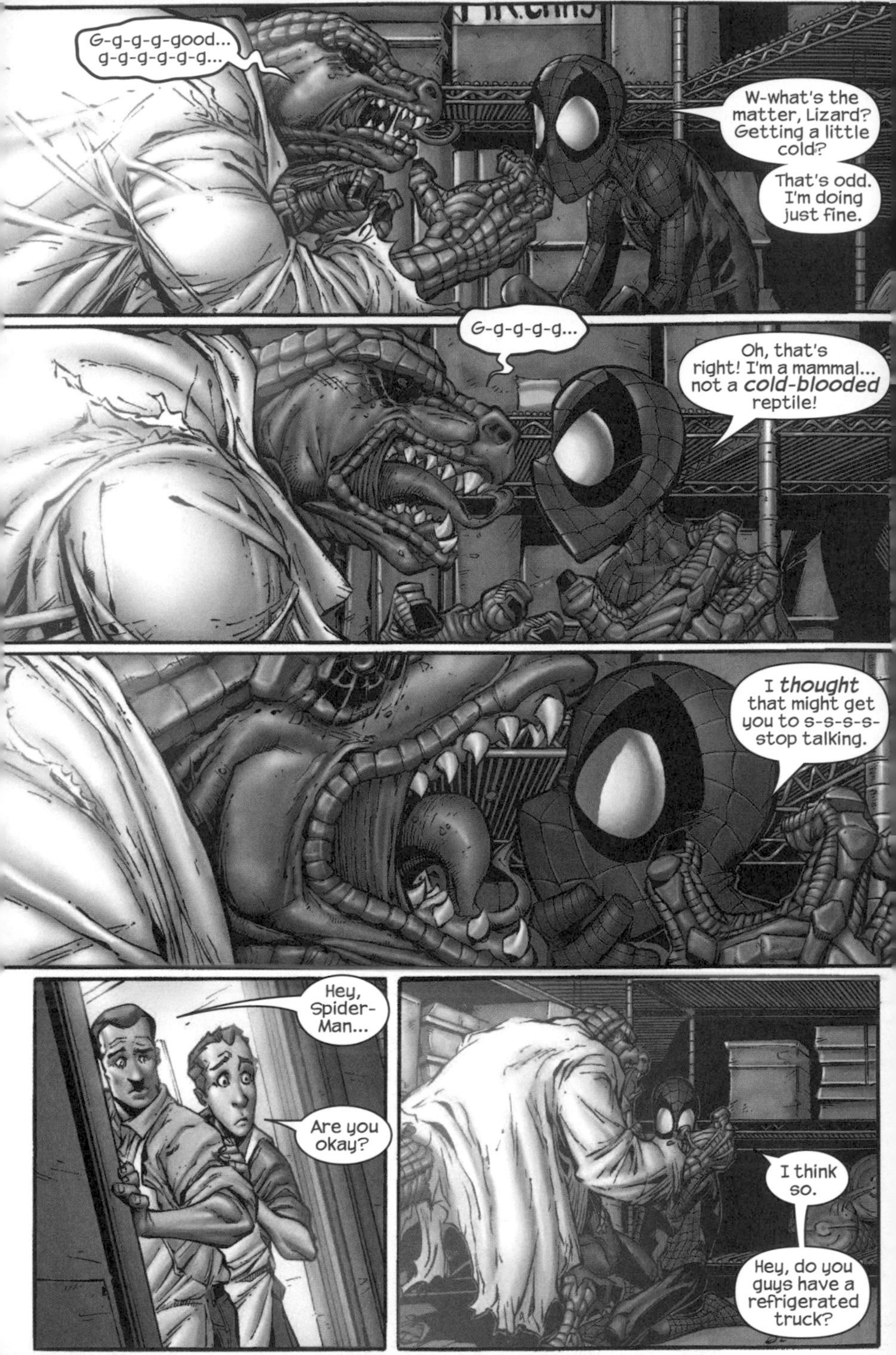

G-g-g-g-good... g-g-g-g-g-g...
W-what's the matter, Lizard? Getting a little cold?
That's odd. I'm doing just fine.
G-g-g-g-g...
Oh, that's right! I'm a mammal... not a *cold-blooded* reptile!
I *thought* that might get you to s-s-s-s-stop talking.
Hey, Spider-Man...
Are you okay?
I think so.
Hey, do you guys have a refrigerated truck?

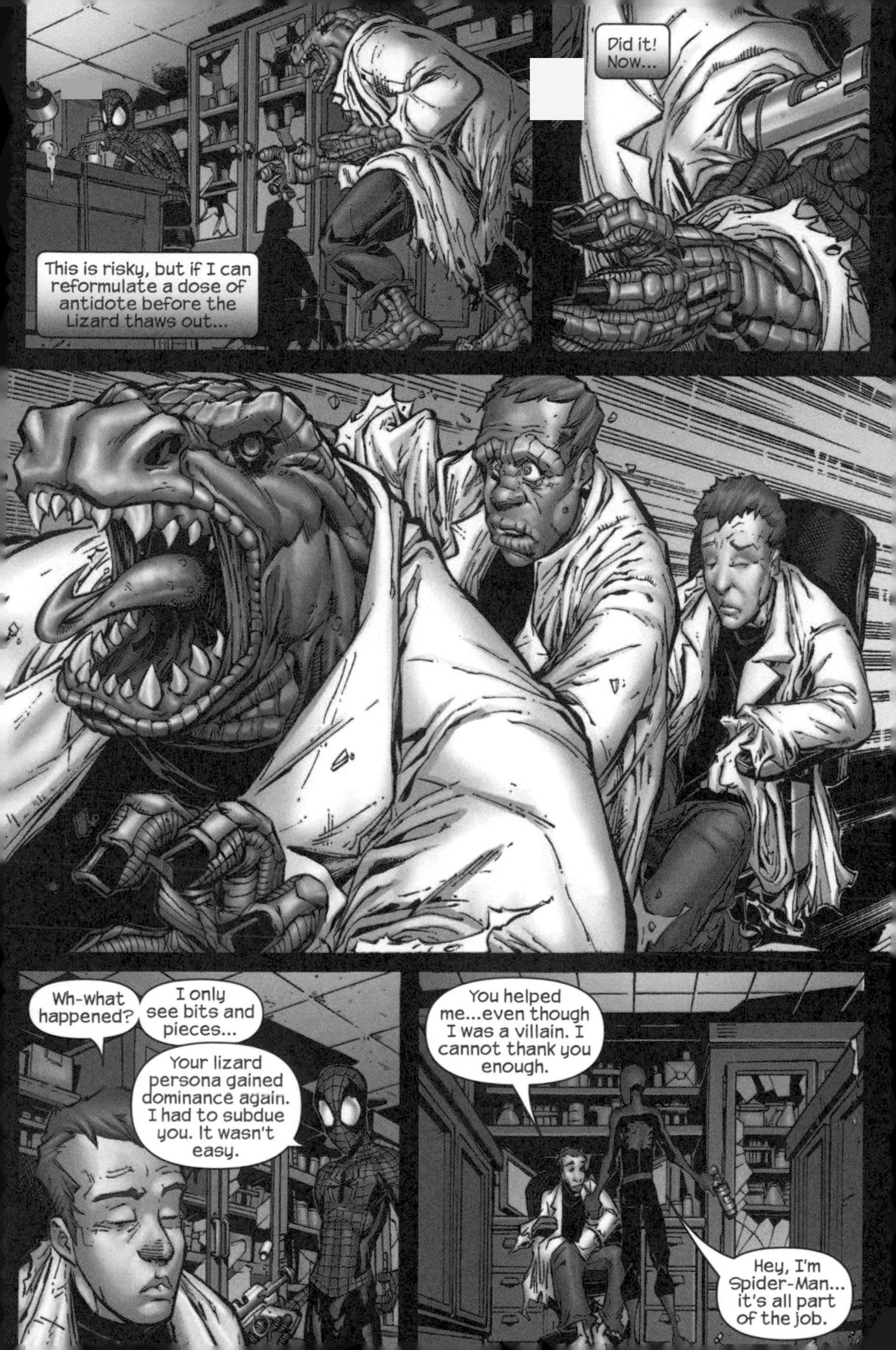
This is risky, but if I can reformulate a dose of antidote before the Lizard thaws out...
Did it! Now...
Wh-what happened?
I only see bits and pieces...
Your lizard persona gained dominance again. I had to subdue you. It wasn't easy.
You helped me...even though I was a villain. I cannot thank you enough.
Hey, I'm Spider-Man... it's all part of the job.

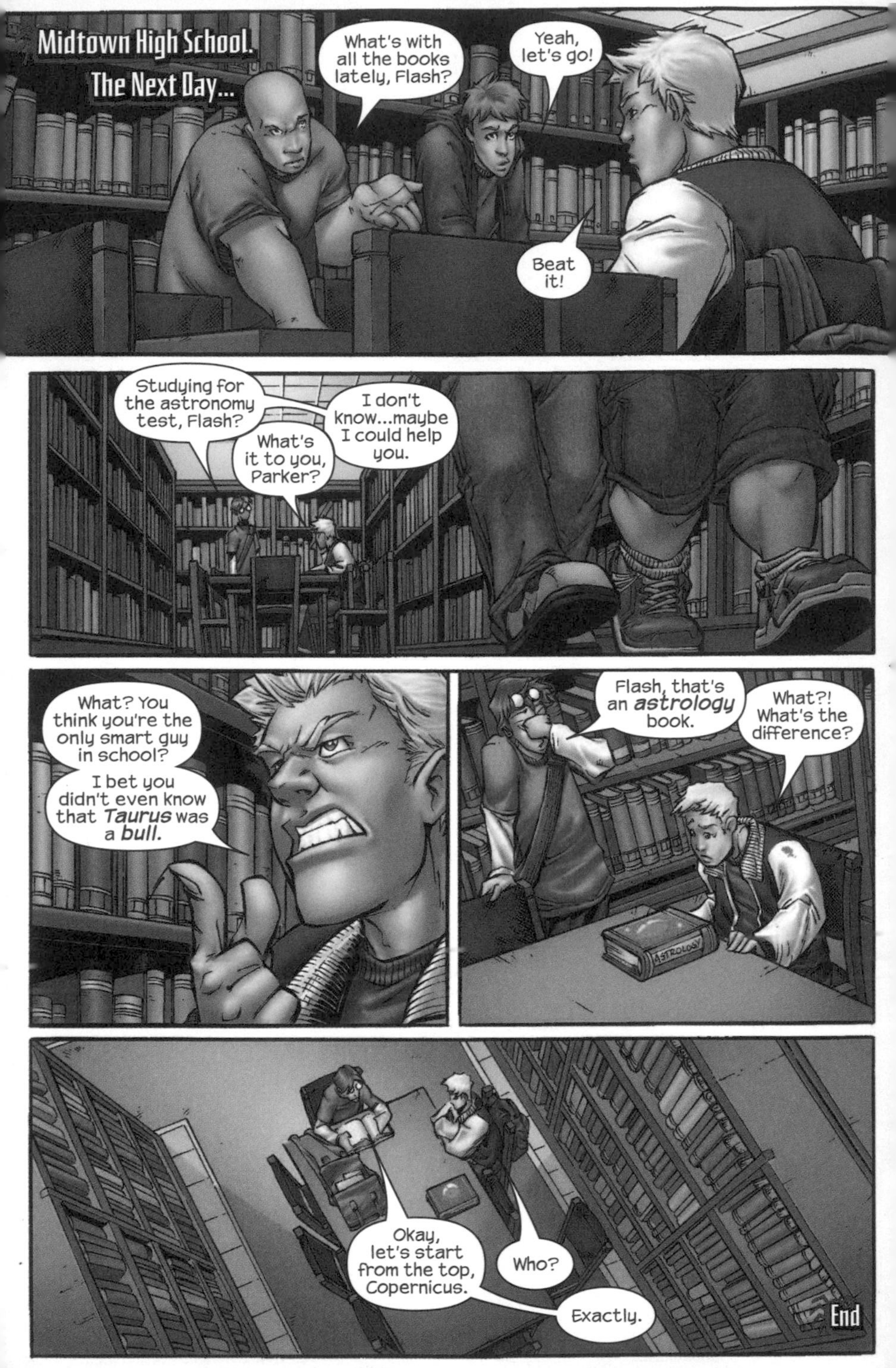

Midtown High School.
The Next Day...
What's with all the books lately, Flash?
Yeah, let's go!
Beat it!
Studying for the astronomy test, Flash?
What's it to you, Parker?
I don't know...maybe I could help you.
What? You think you're the only smart guy in school?
I bet you didn't even know that *Taurus* was a ***bull.***
Flash, that's an ***astrology*** book.
What?! What's the difference?
ASTROLOGY
Okay, let's start from the top, Copernicus.
Who?
Exactly.
End

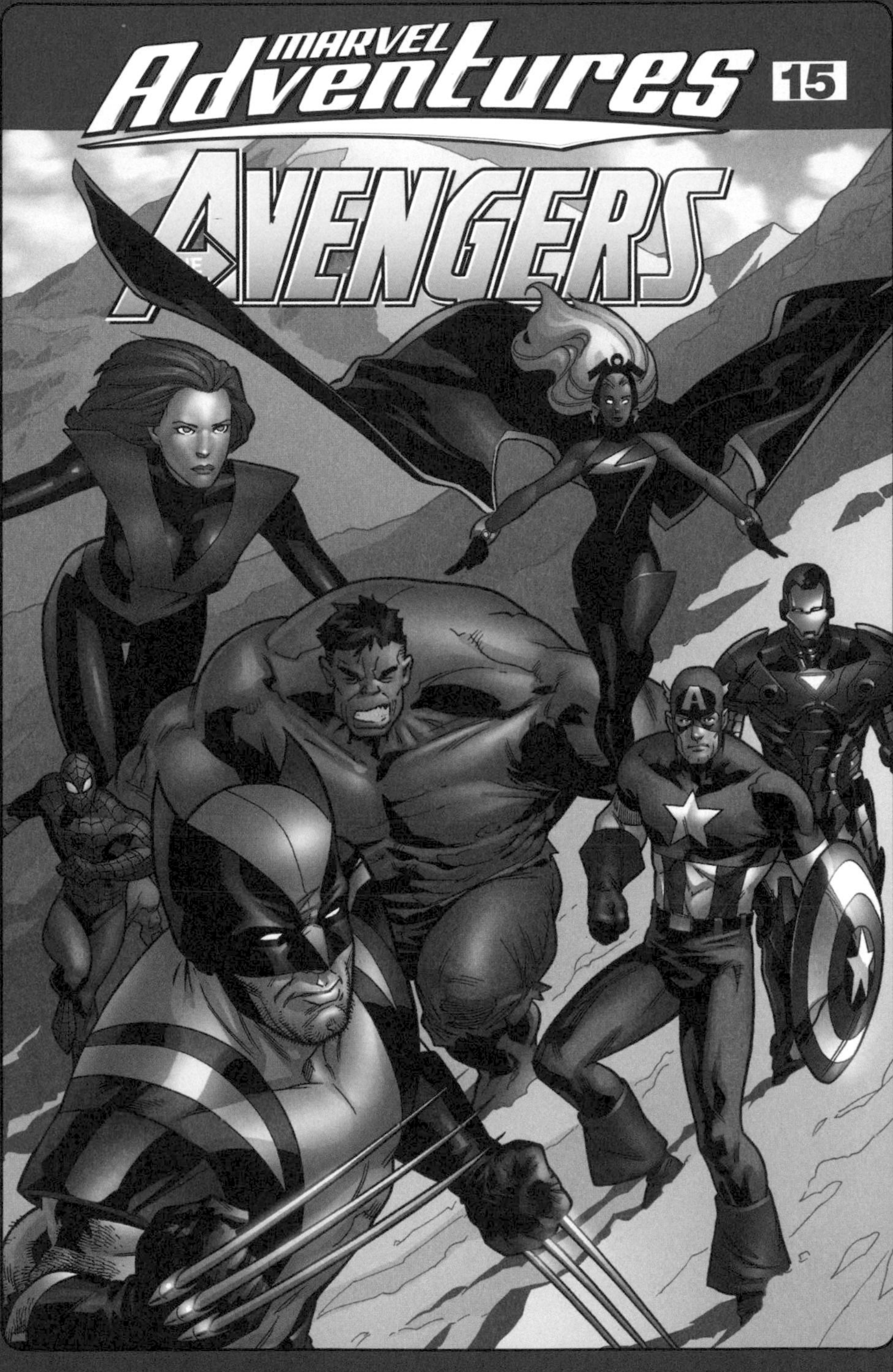
MARVEL
Adventures
15
AVENGERS

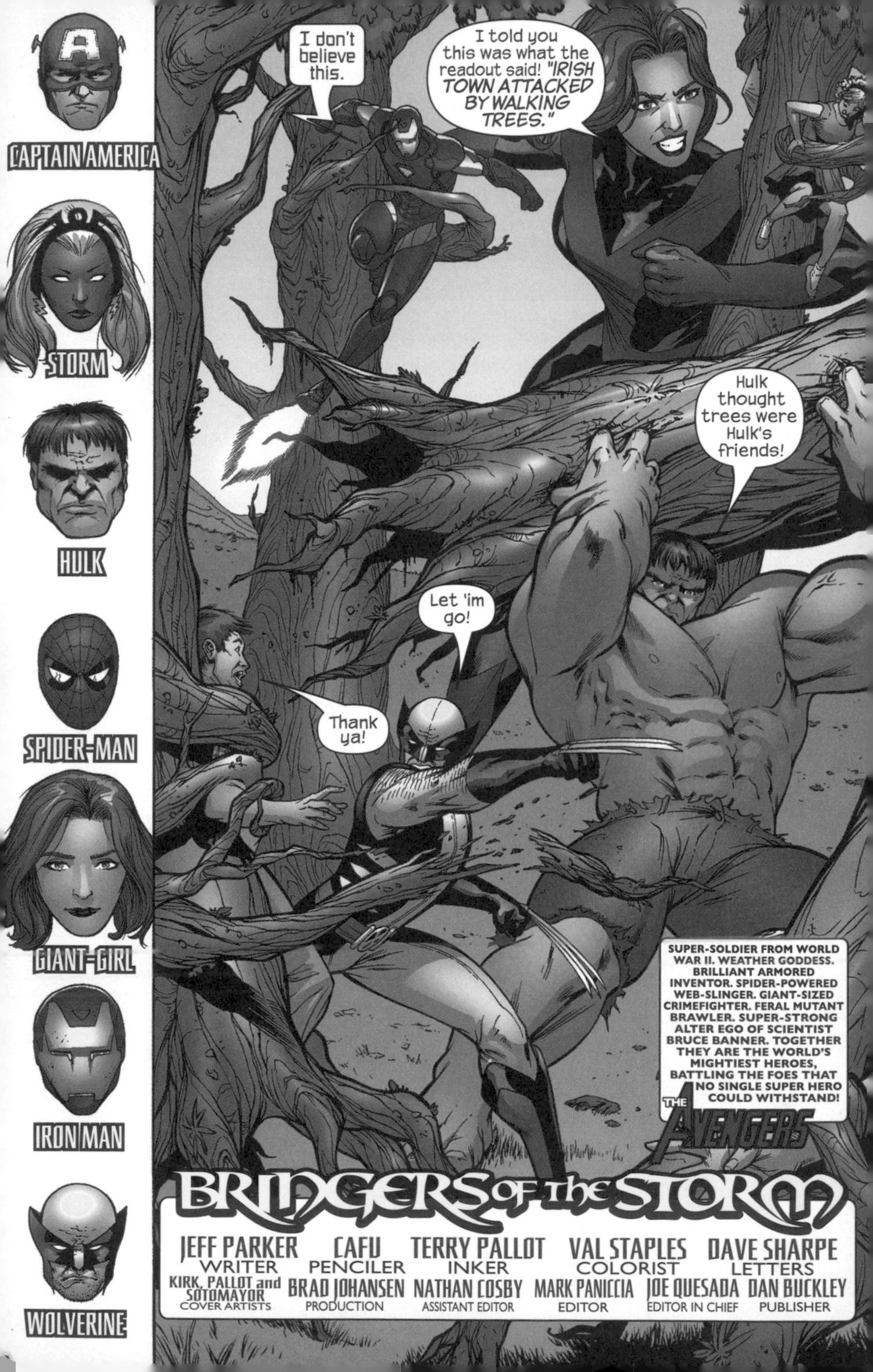

CAPTAIN AMERICA
STORM
HULK
SPIDER-MAN
GIANT-GIRL
IRON MAN
WOLVERINE
I don't believe this.
I told you this was what the readout said! "IRISH TOWN ATTACKED BY WALKING TREES."
Hulk thought trees were Hulk's friends!
Let 'im go!
Thank ya!
SUPER-SOLDIER FROM WORLD WAR II. WEATHER GODDESS. BRILLIANT ARMORED INVENTOR. SPIDER-POWERED WEB-SLINGER. GIANT-SIZED CRIMEFIGHTER. FERAL MUTANT BRAWLER. SUPER-STRONG ALTER EGO OF SCIENTIST BRUCE BANNER. TOGETHER THEY ARE THE WORLD'S MIGHTIEST HEROES, BATTLING THE FOES THAT NO SINGLE SUPER HERO COULD WITHSTAND!
THE AVENGERS
BRINGERS OF THE STORM
JEFF PARKER WRITER
CAFU PENCILER
TERRY PALLOT INKER
VAL STAPLES COLORIST
DAVE SHARPE LETTERS
KIRK, PALLOT and SOTOMAYOR COVER ARTISTS
BRAD JOHANSEN PRODUCTION
NATHAN COSBY ASSISTANT EDITOR
MARK PANICCIA EDITOR
JOE QUESADA EDITOR IN CHIEF
DAN BUCKLEY PUBLISHER

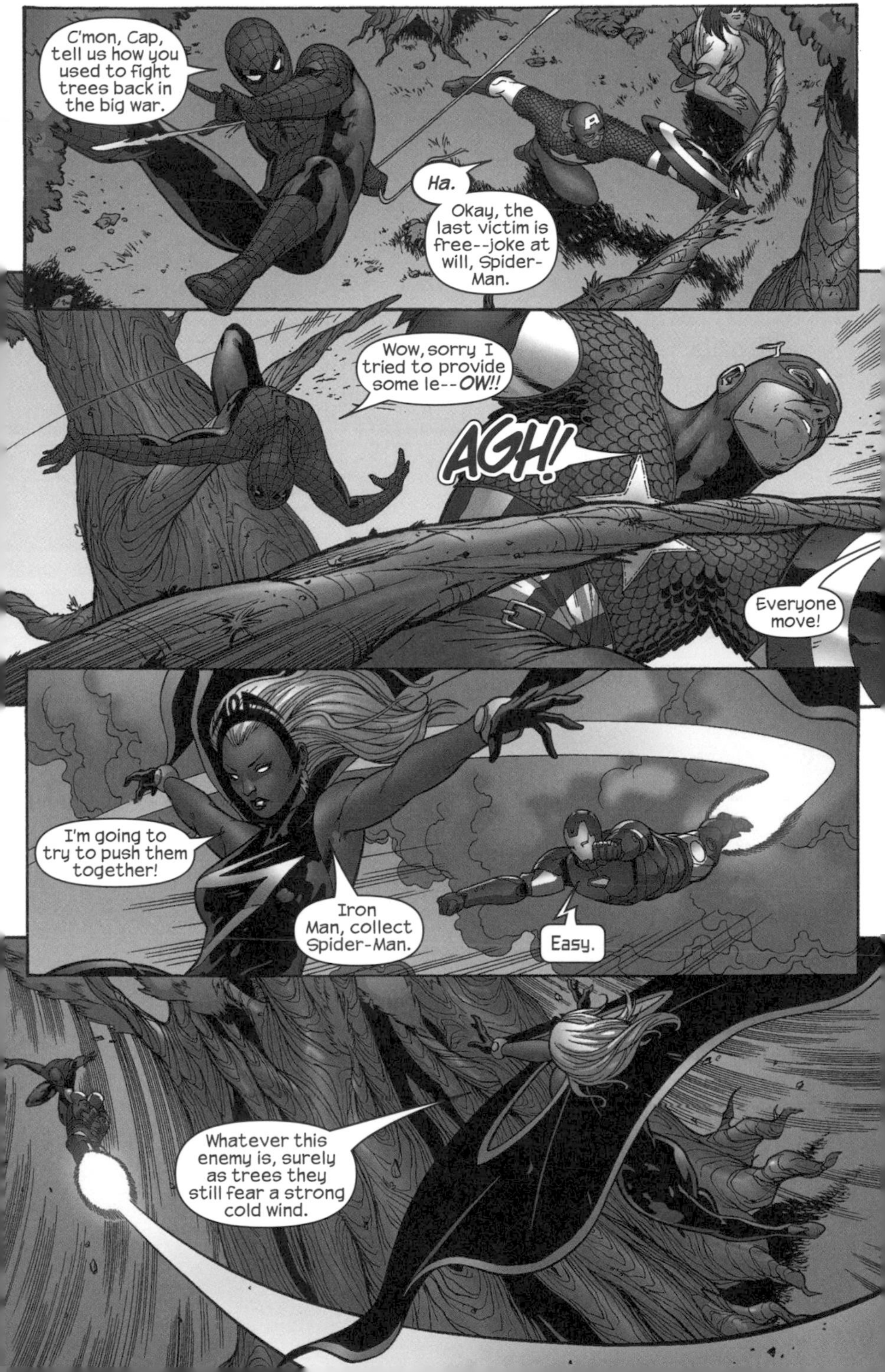
C'mon, Cap, tell us how you used to fight trees back in the big war.
Ha.
Okay, the last victim is free--joke at will, Spider-Man.
Wow, sorry I tried to provide some le--OW!!
AGH!
Everyone move!
I'm going to try to push them together!
Iron Man, collect Spider-Man.
Easy.
Whatever this enemy is, surely as trees they still fear a strong cold wind.

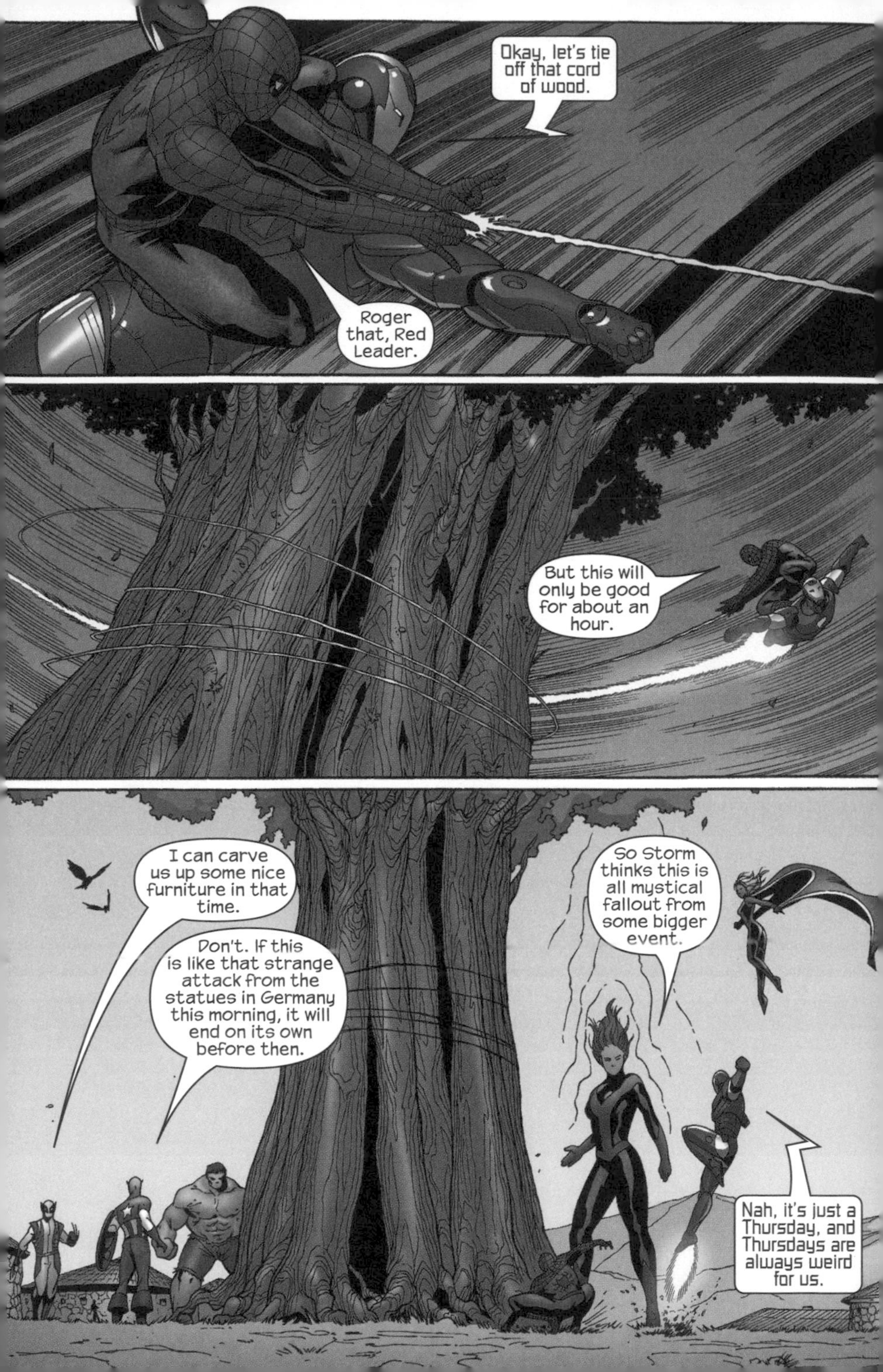
Okay, let's tie off that cord of wood.
Roger that, Red Leader.
But this will only be good for about an hour.
I can carve us up some nice furniture in that time.
Don't. If this is like that strange attack from the statues in Germany this morning, it will end on its own before then.
So Storm thinks this is all mystical fallout from some bigger event.
Nah, it's just a Thursday, and Thursdays are always weird for us.

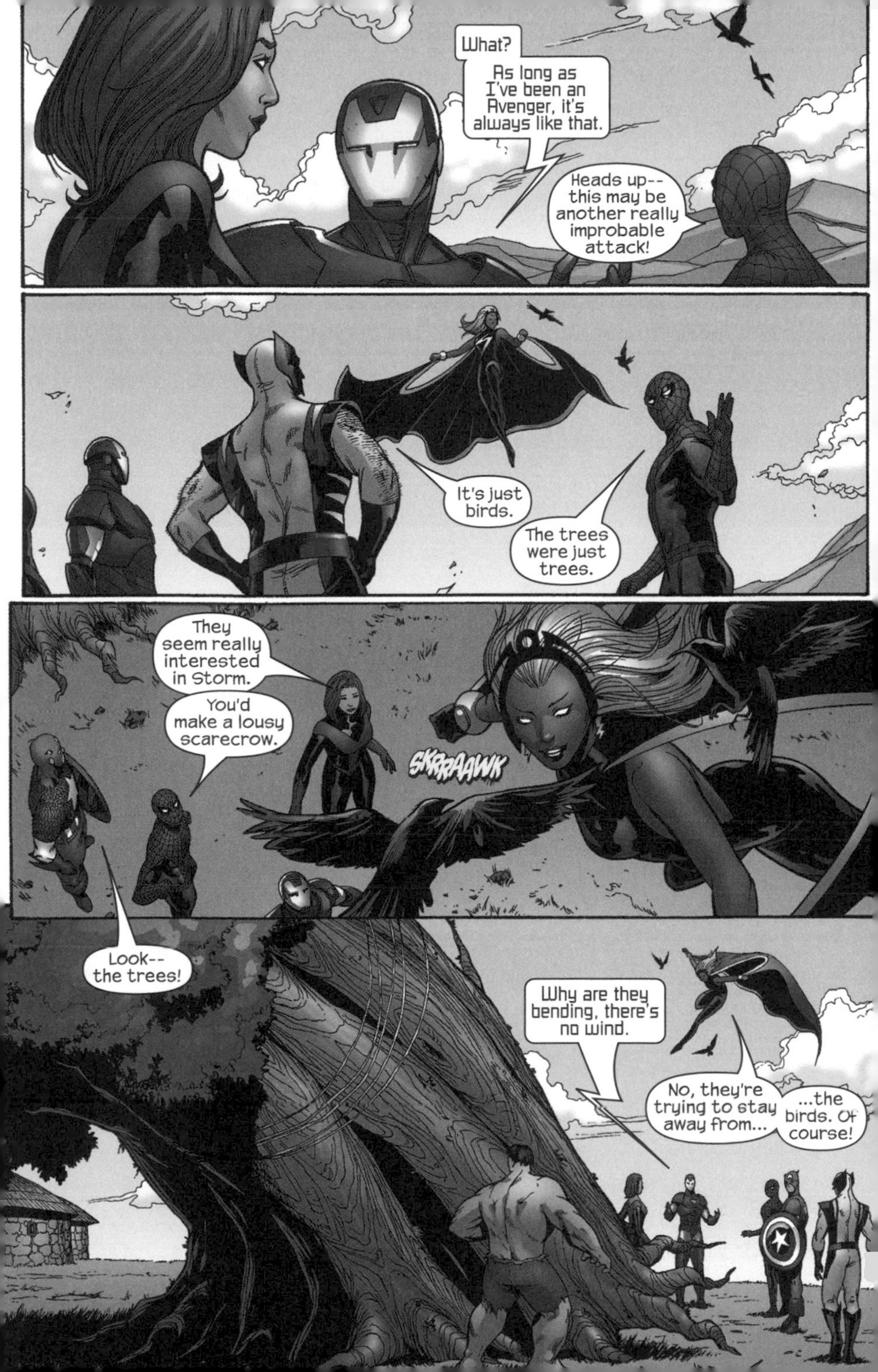
What?
As long as I've been an Avenger, it's always like that.
Heads up-- this may be another really improbable attack!
It's just birds.
The trees were just trees.
They seem really interested in Storm.
You'd make a lousy scarecrow.
SKRRAAWK
Look-- the trees!
Why are they bending, there's no wind.
No, they're trying to stay away from...
...the birds. Of course!

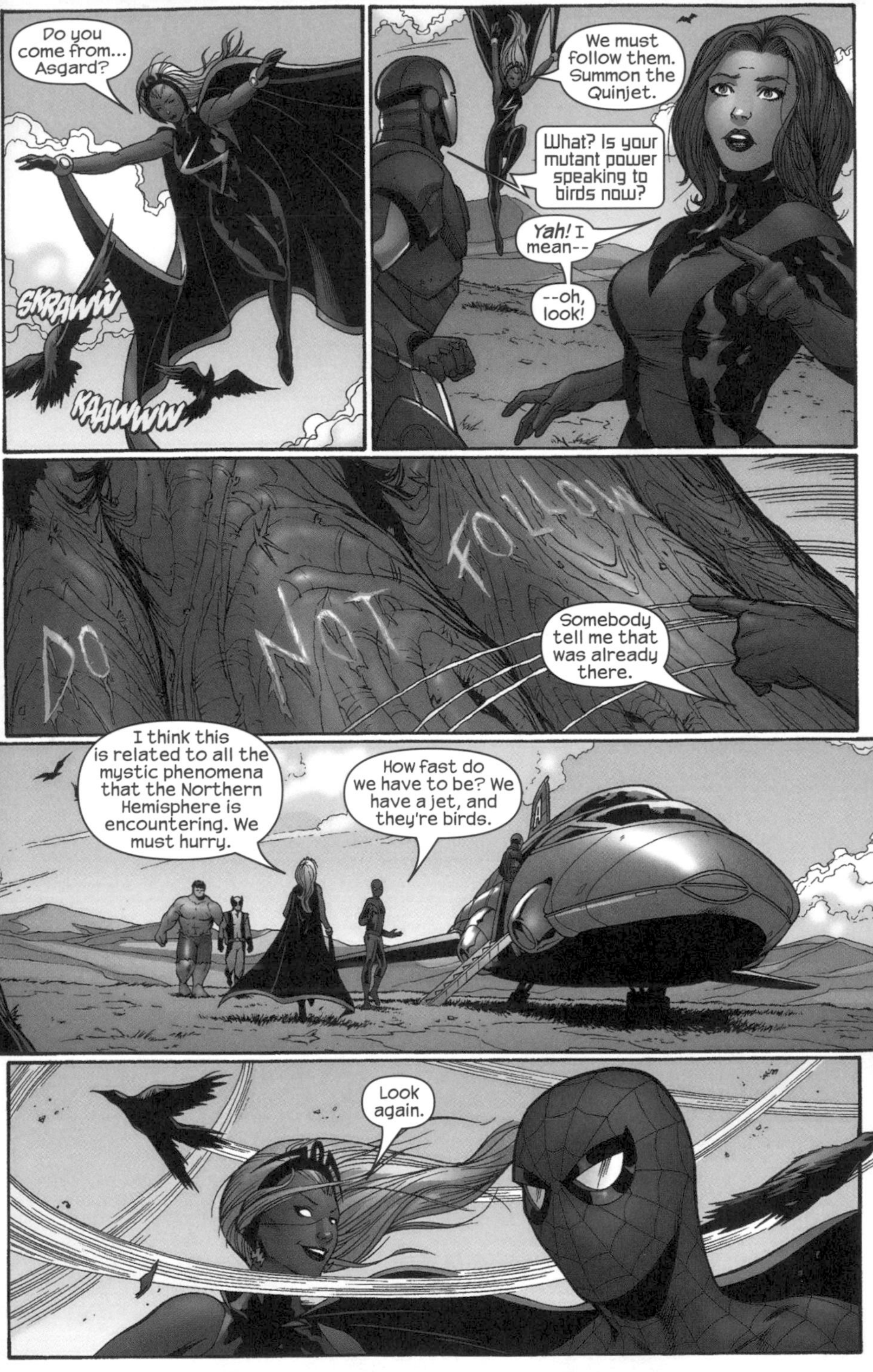

Do you come from... Asgard?
SKRAWW
KAAWWW
We must follow them. Summon the Quinjet.
What? Is your mutant power speaking to birds now?
Yah! I mean--
--oh, look!
DO NOT FOLLOW
Somebody tell me that was already there.
I think this is related to all the mystic phenomena that the Northern Hemisphere is encountering. We must hurry.
How fast do we have to be? We have a jet, and they're birds.
Look again.

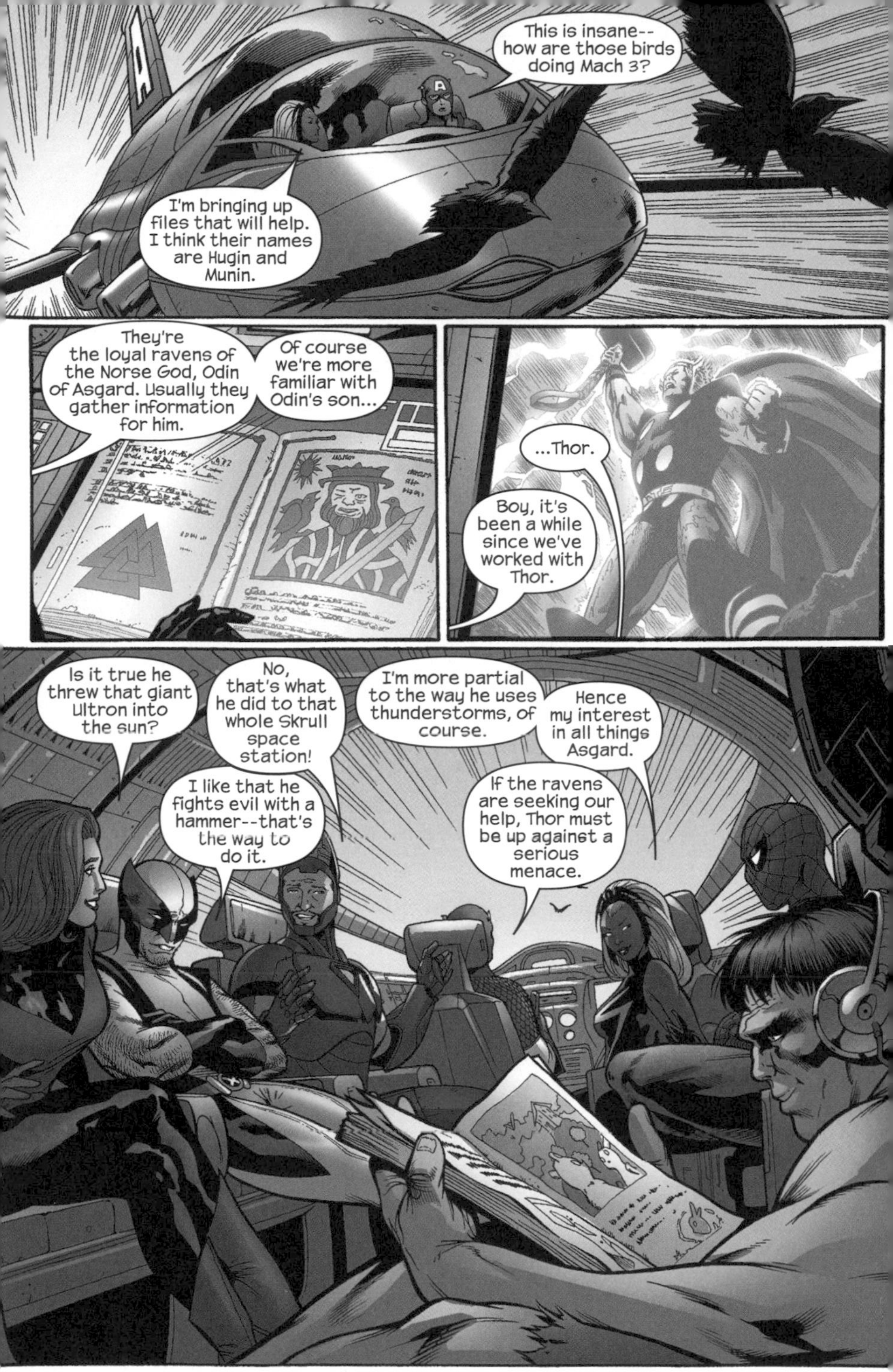
This is insane--how are those birds doing Mach 3?
I'm bringing up files that will help. I think their names are Hugin and Munin.
They're the loyal ravens of the Norse God, Odin of Asgard. Usually they gather information for him.
Of course we're more familiar with Odin's son...
...Thor.
Boy, it's been a while since we've worked with Thor.
Is it true he threw that giant Ultron into the sun?
No, that's what he did to that whole Skrull space station!
I like that he fights evil with a hammer--that's the way to do it.
I'm more partial to the way he uses thunderstorms, of course.
Hence my interest in all things Asgard.
If the ravens are seeking our help, Thor must be up against a serious menace.

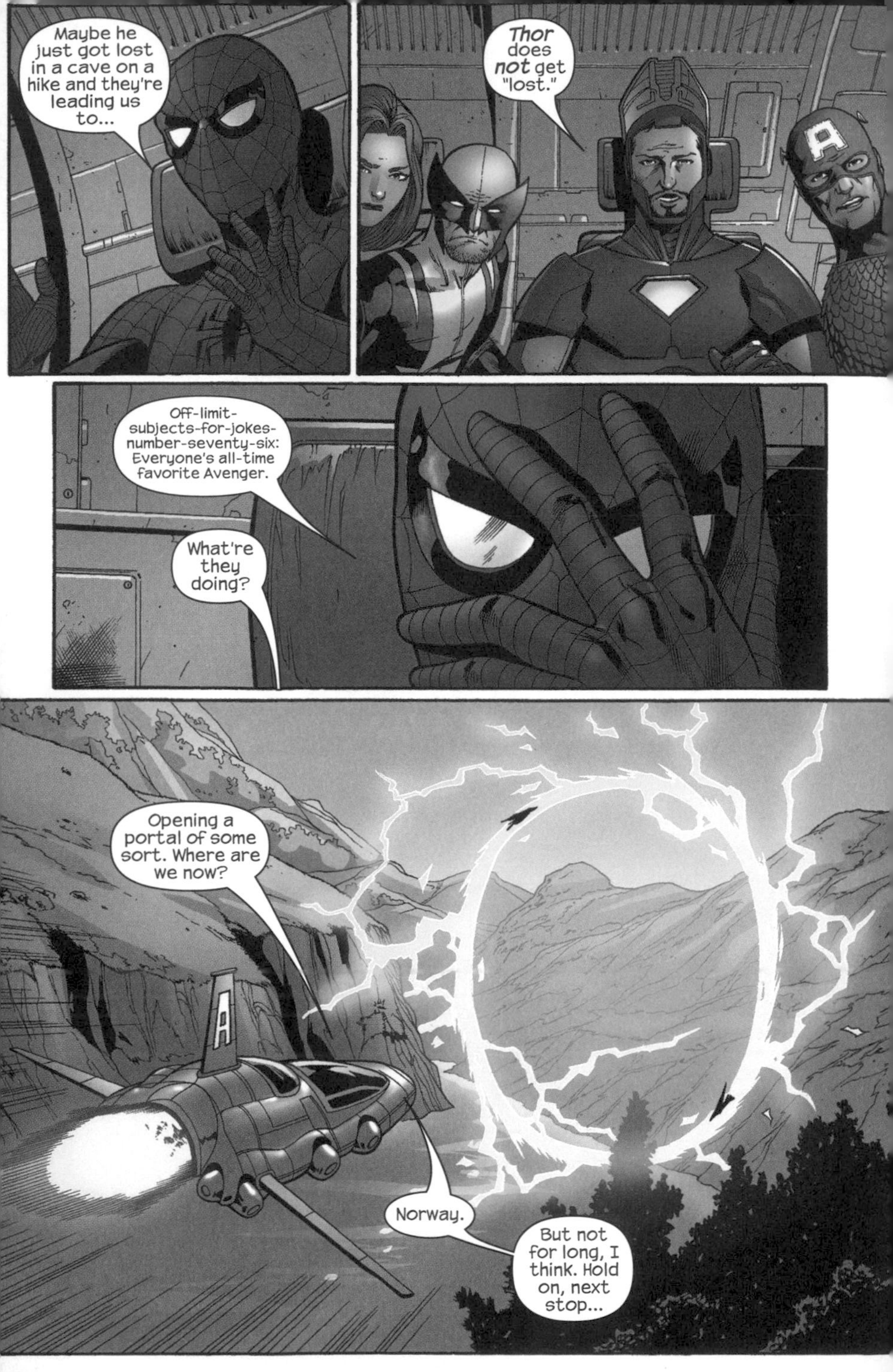
Maybe he just got lost in a cave on a hike and they're leading us to...
Thor does *not* get "lost."
Off-limit-subjects-for-jokes-number-seventy-six: Everyone's all-time favorite Avenger.
What're they doing?
Opening a portal of some sort. Where are we now?
Norway.
But not for long, I think. Hold on, next stop...

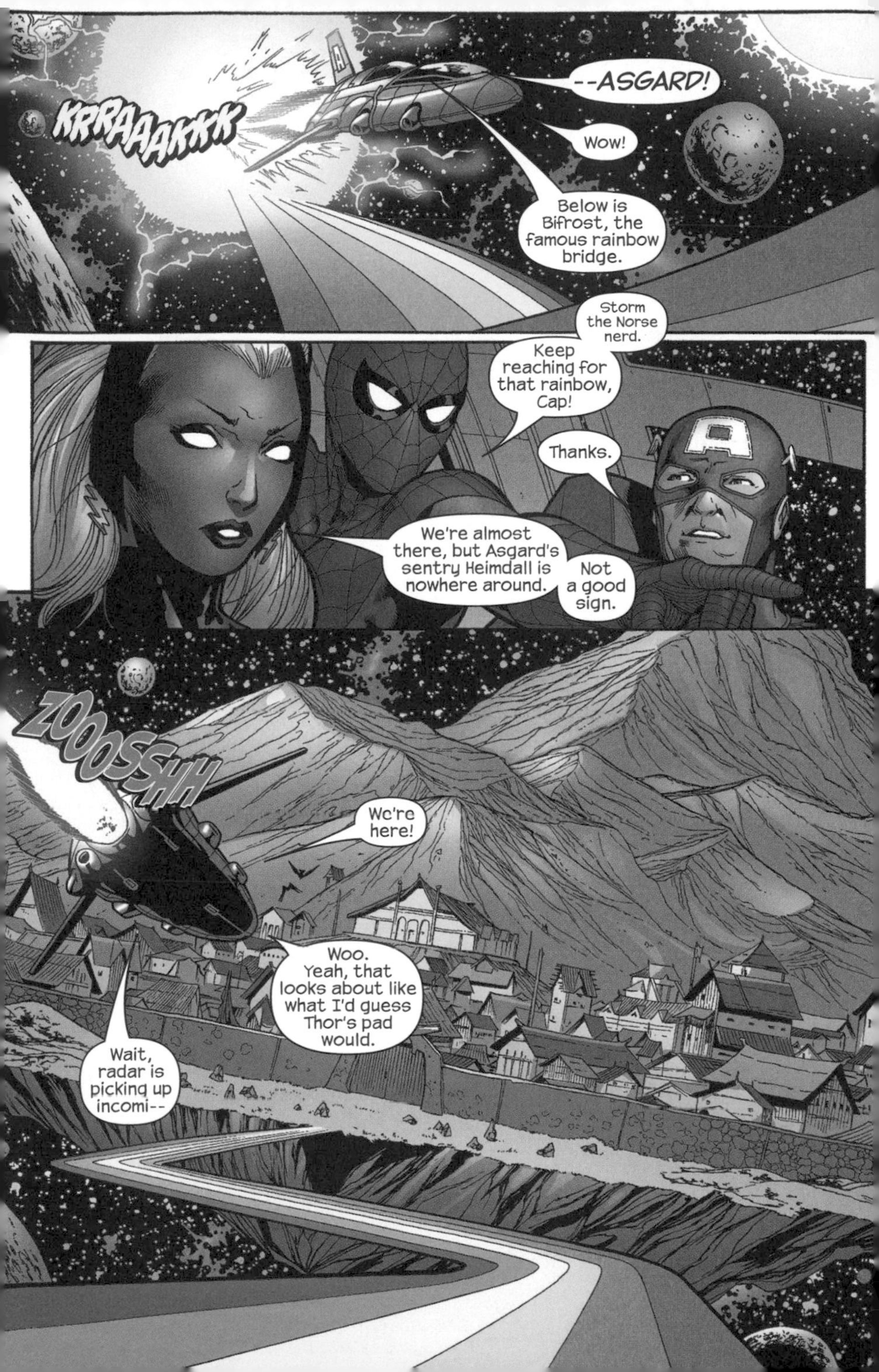
KRRAAAKKK
--ASGARD!
Wow!
Below is Bifrost, the famous rainbow bridge.
Storm the Norse nerd.
Keep reaching for that rainbow, Cap!
Thanks.
We're almost there, but Asgard's sentry Heimdall is nowhere around.
Not a good sign.
ZOOOSSHH
We're here!
Woo. Yeah, that looks about like what I'd guess Thor's pad would.
Wait, radar is picking up incomi--

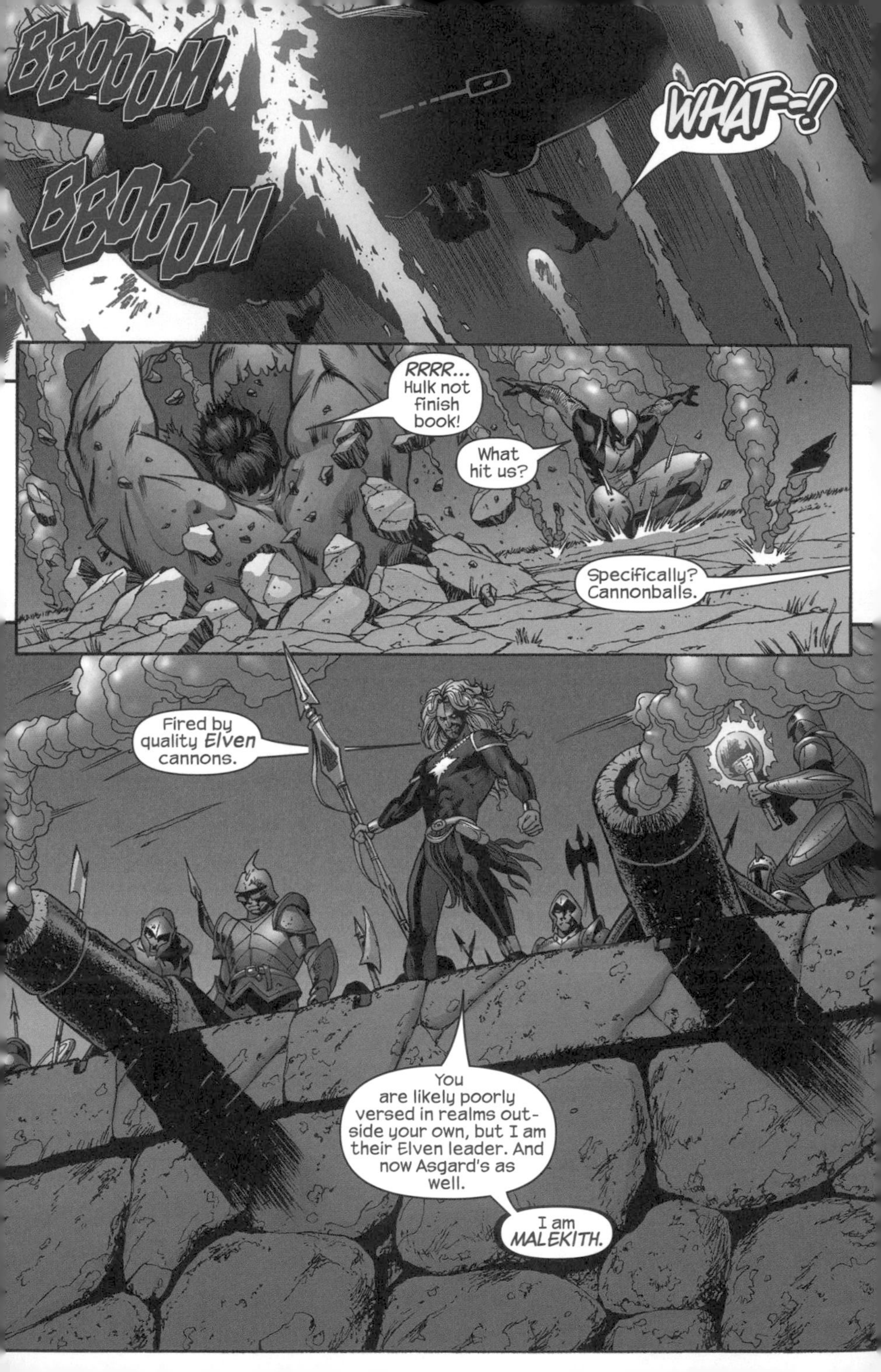
BBOOOOM
BBOOOOM
WHAT--!
RRRR... Hulk not finish book!
What hit us?
Specifically? Cannonballs.
Fired by quality Elven cannons.
You are likely poorly versed in realms out-side your own, but I am their Elven leader. And now Asgard's as well.
I am MALEKITH.

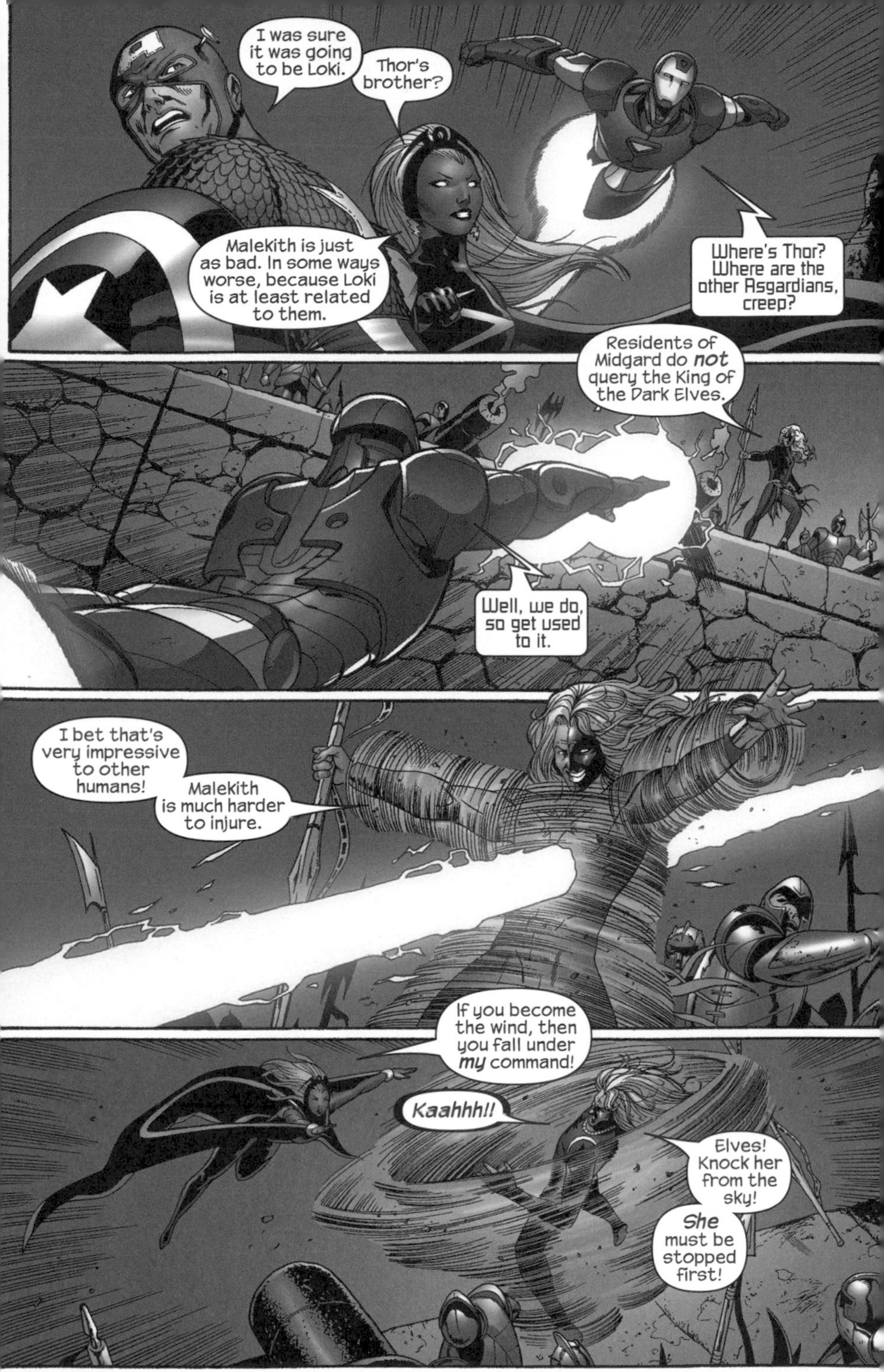

I was sure it was going to be Loki.
Thor's brother?
Malekith is just as bad. In some ways worse, because Loki is at least related to them.
Where's Thor? Where are the other Asgardians, creep?
Residents of Midgard do *not* query the King of the Dark Elves.
Well, we do, so get used to it.
I bet that's very impressive to other humans!
Malekith is much harder to injure.
If you become the wind, then you fall under *my* command!
Kaahhh!!
Elves! Knock her from the sky!
She must be stopped first!

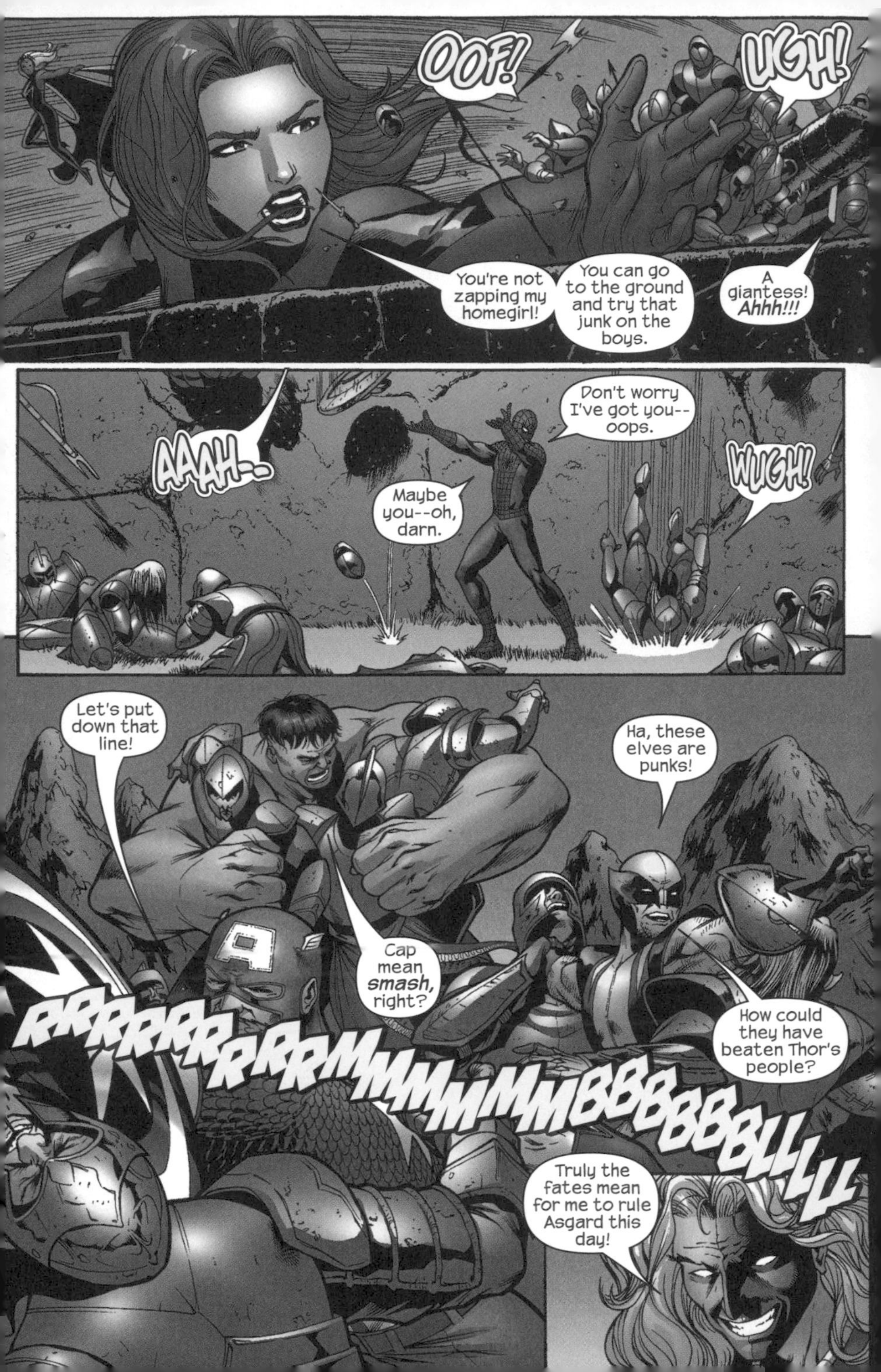

OOF!
UGH!
You're not zapping my homegirl!
You can go to the ground and try that junk on the boys.
A giantess! Ahhh!!!
AAAH--
Don't worry I've got you-- oops.
WUGH!
Maybe you--oh, darn.
Let's put down that line!
Ha, these elves are punks!
Cap mean smash, right?
How could they have beaten Thor's people?
RRRRRRRRRMMMMMMMMBBBBBBLLLL
Truly the fates mean for me to rule Asgard this day!

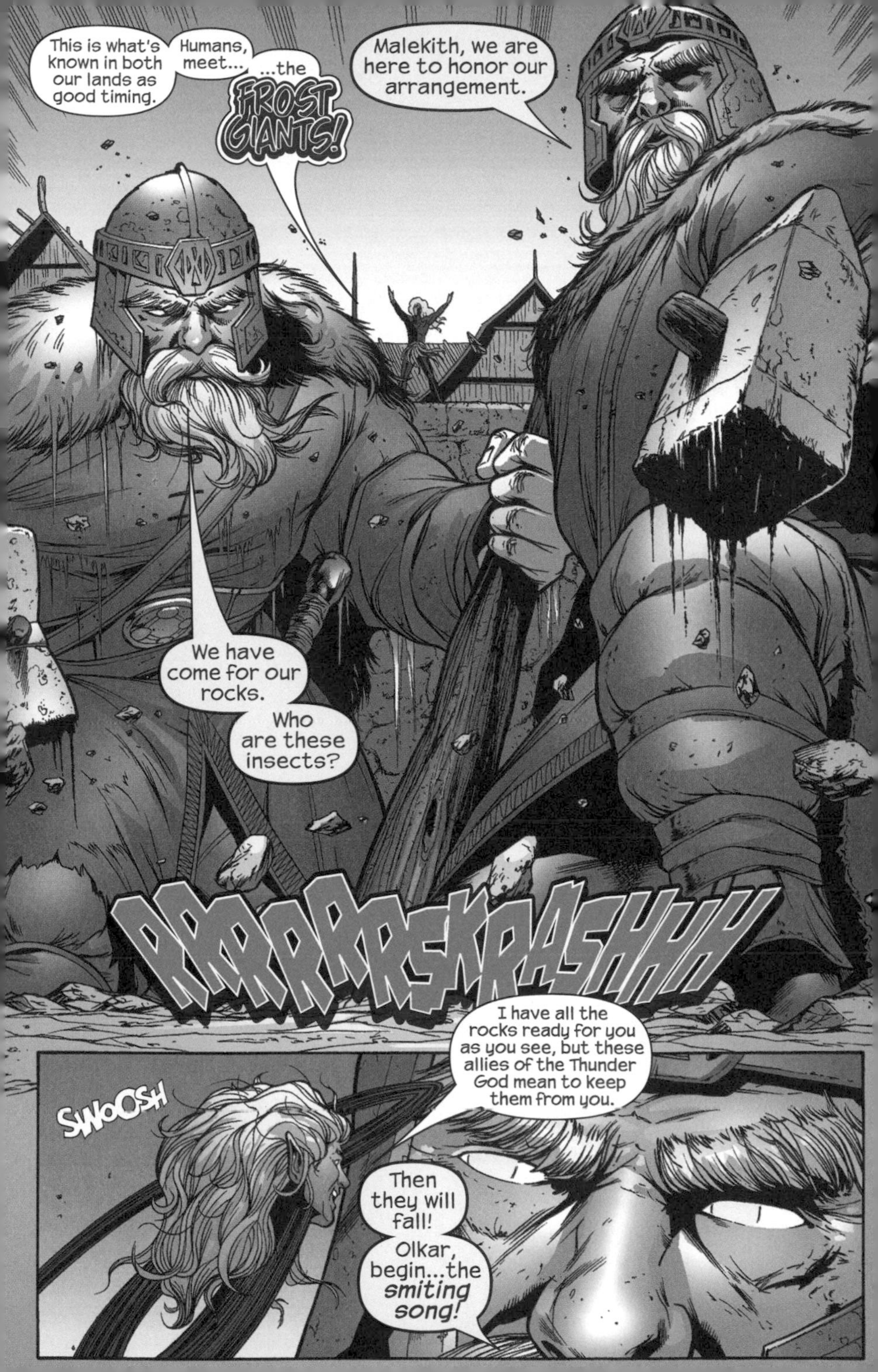
This is what's known in both our lands as good timing.
Humans, meet...
...the FROST GIANTS!
Malekith, we are here to honor our arrangement.
We have come for our rocks.
Who are these insects?
RRRRRRRSKRASHHH
SWOOSH
I have all the rocks ready for you as you see, but these allies of the Thunder God mean to keep them from you.
Then they will fall!
Olkar, begin...the *smiting song!*

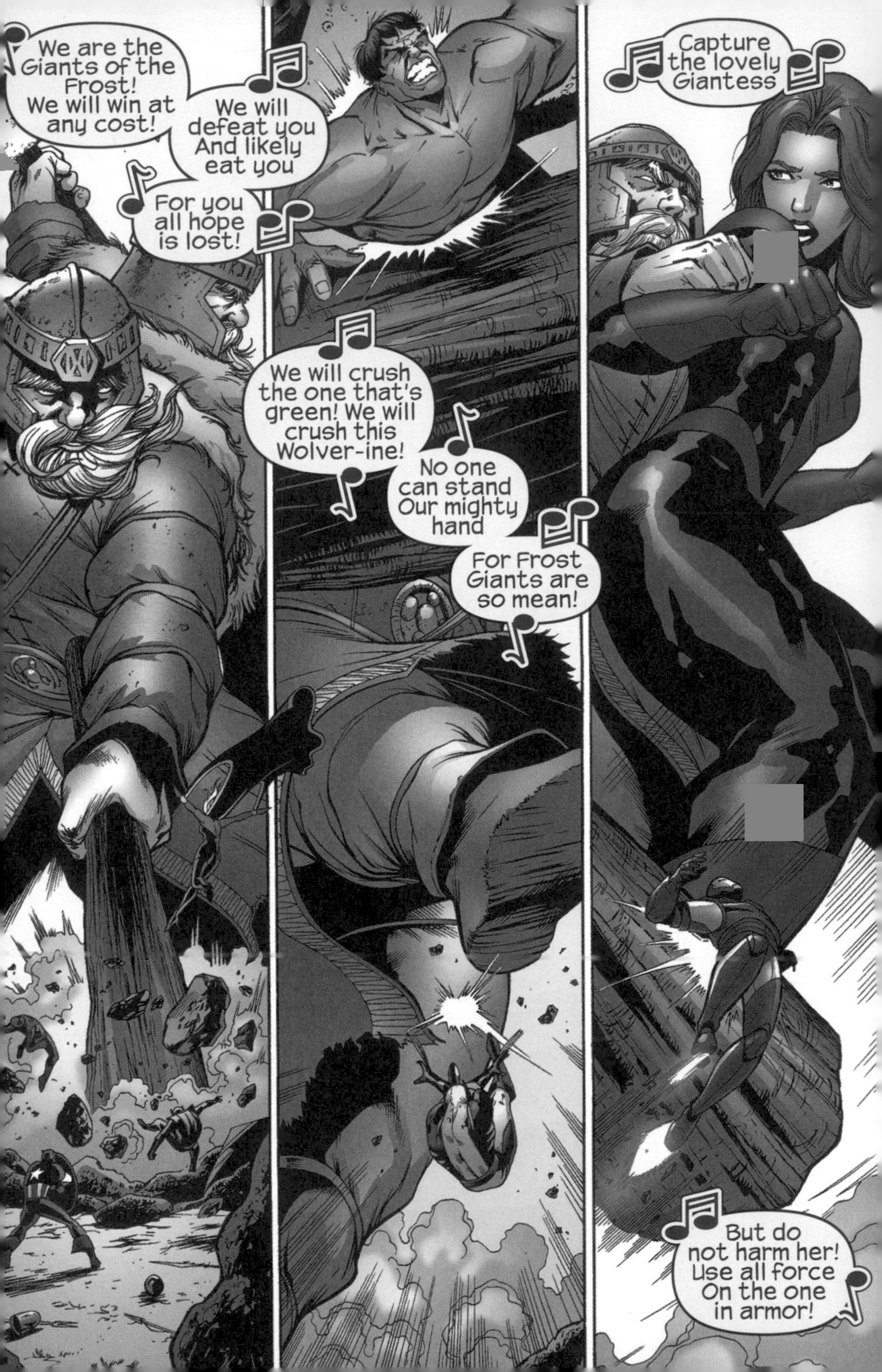
We are the Giants of the Frost! We will win at any cost!
We will defeat you And likely eat you
For you all hope is lost!
We will crush the one that's green! We will crush this Wolver-ine!
No one can stand Our mighty hand
For Frost Giants are so mean!
Capture the lovely Giantess
But do not harm her! Use all force On the one in armor!

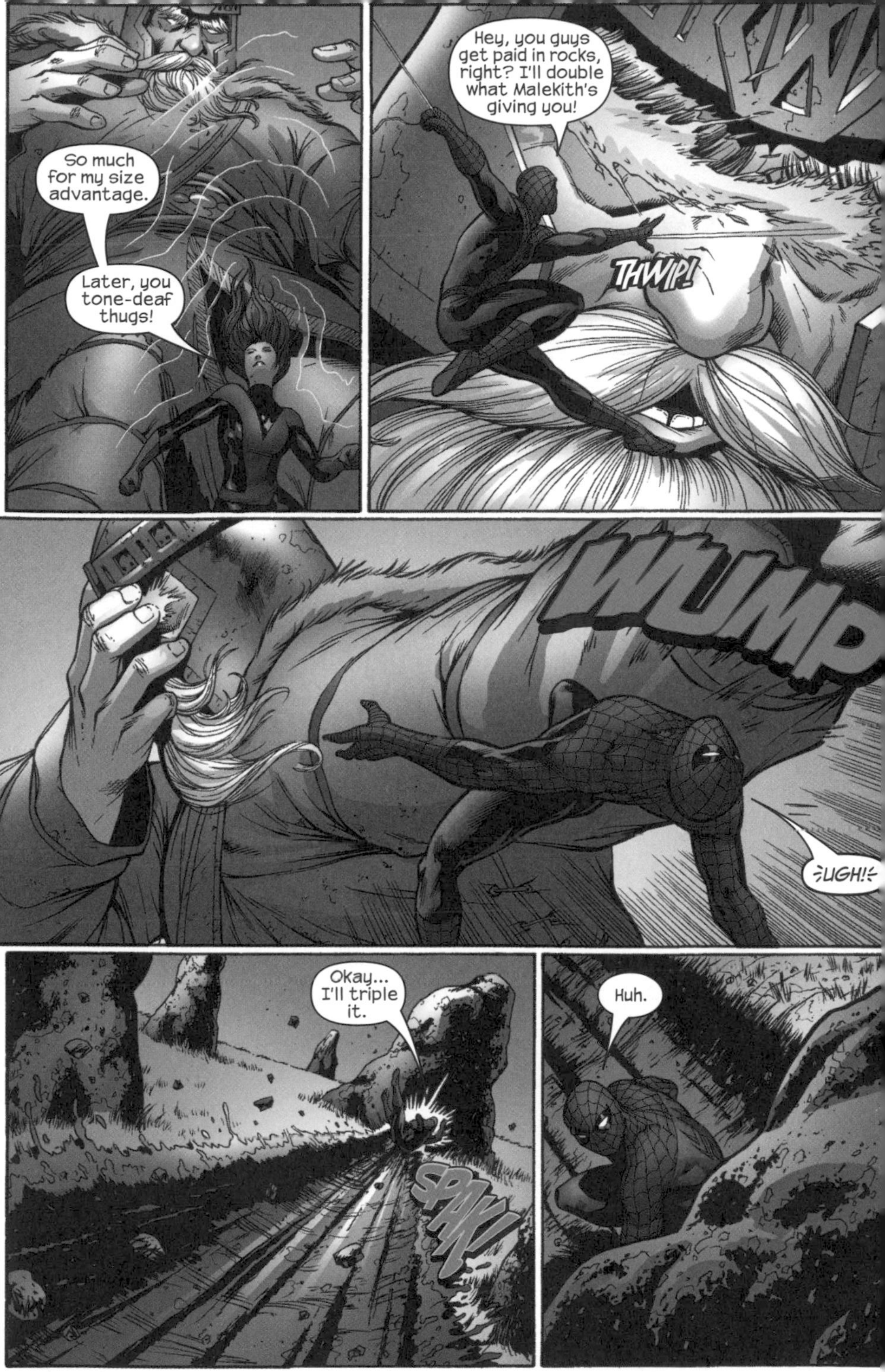
So much for my size advantage.
Later, you tone-deaf thugs!
Hey, you guys get paid in rocks, right? I'll double what Malekith's giving you!
THWIP!
WUMP
UGH!
Okay... I'll triple it.
SPAK!
Huh.

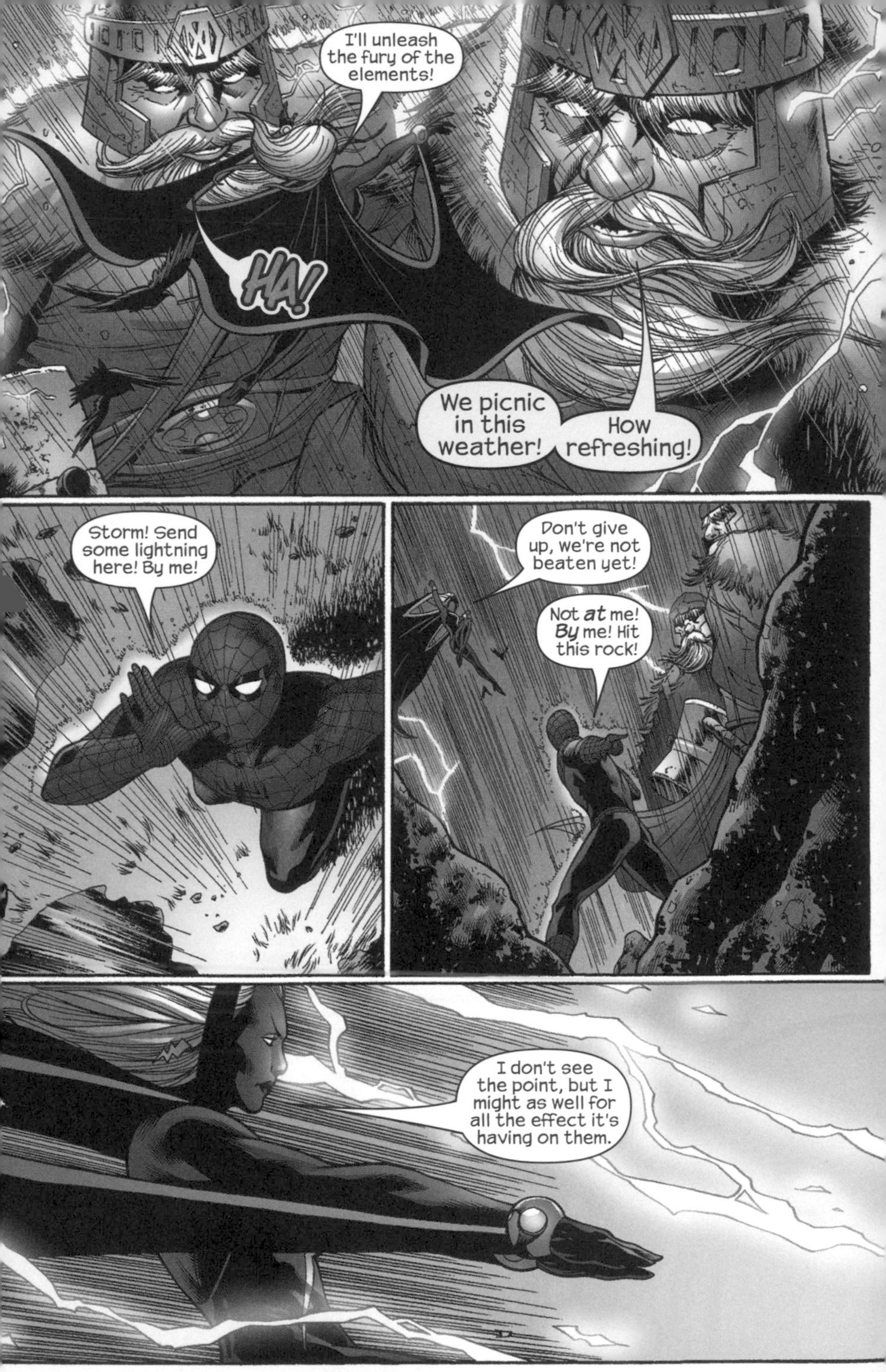
I'll unleash the fury of the elements!
HA!
We picnic in this weather!
How refreshing!
Storm! Send some lightning here! By me!
Don't give up, we're not beaten yet!
Not *at* me! *By* me! Hit this rock!
I don't see the point, but I might as well for all the effect it's having on them.

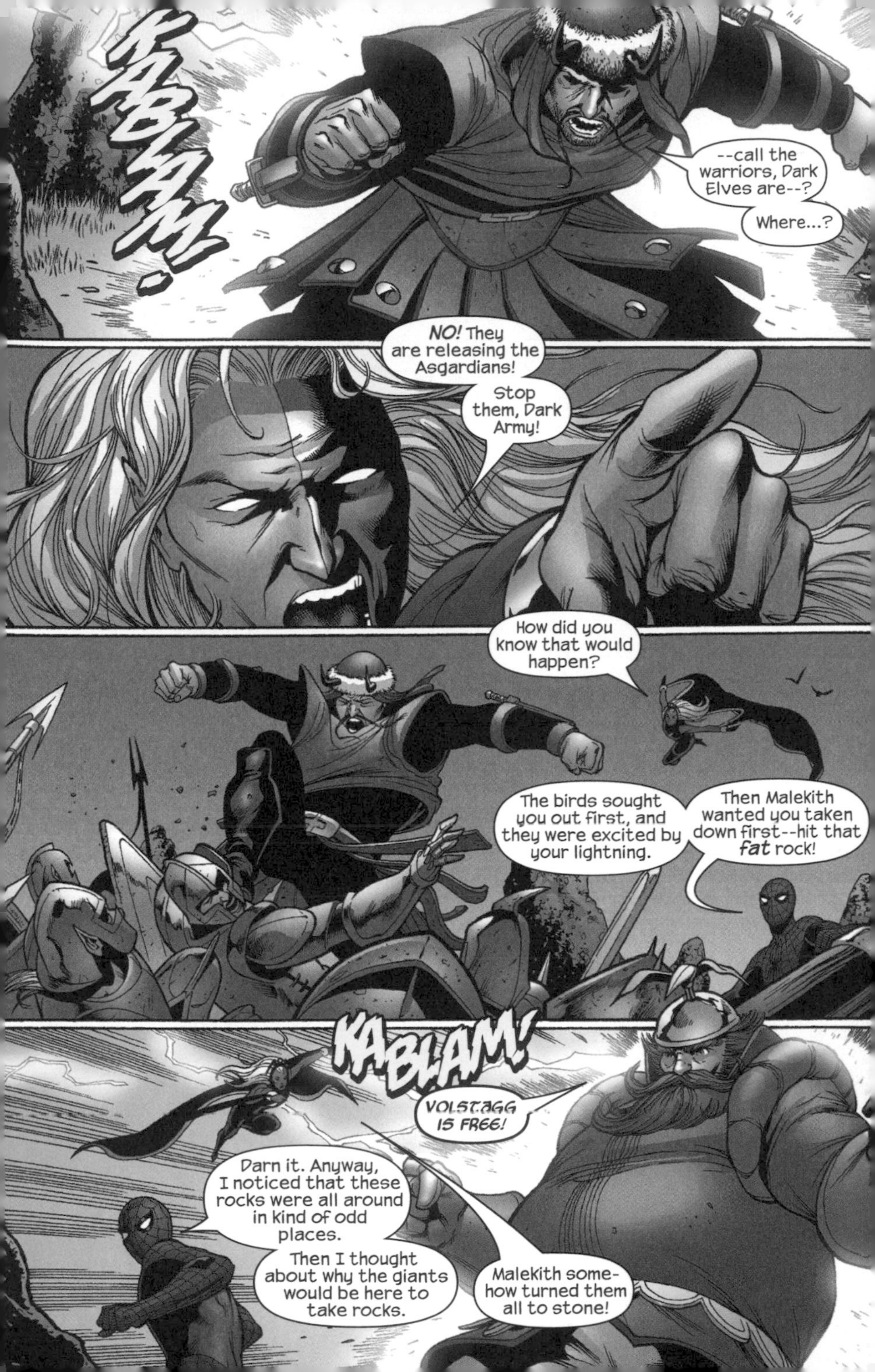
KABLAM!
--call the warriors, Dark Elves are--?
Where...?
NO! They are releasing the Asgardians!
Stop them, Dark Army!
How did you know that would happen?
The birds sought you out first, and they were excited by your lightning.
Then Malekith wanted you taken down first--hit that fat rock!
KABLAM!
VOLSTAGG IS FREE!
Darn it. Anyway, I noticed that these rocks were all around in kind of odd places.
Then I thought about why the giants would be here to take rocks.
Malekith somehow turned them all to stone!

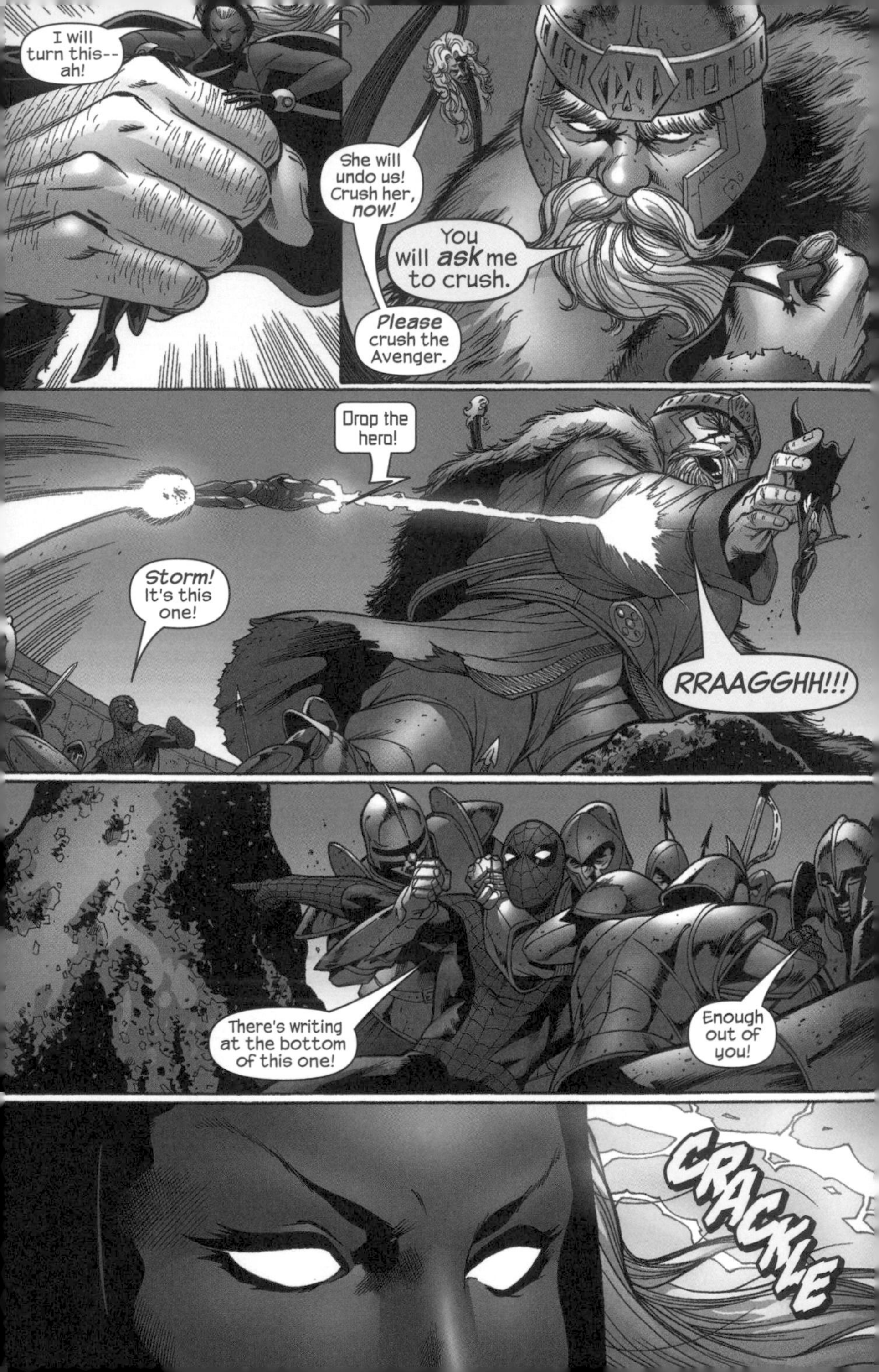
I will turn this-- ah!
She will undo us! Crush her, *now!*
You will **ask** me to crush.
Please crush the Avenger.
Drop the hero!
Storm! It's this one!
RRAAGGHH!!!
There's writing at the bottom of this one!
Enough out of you!
CRACKLE

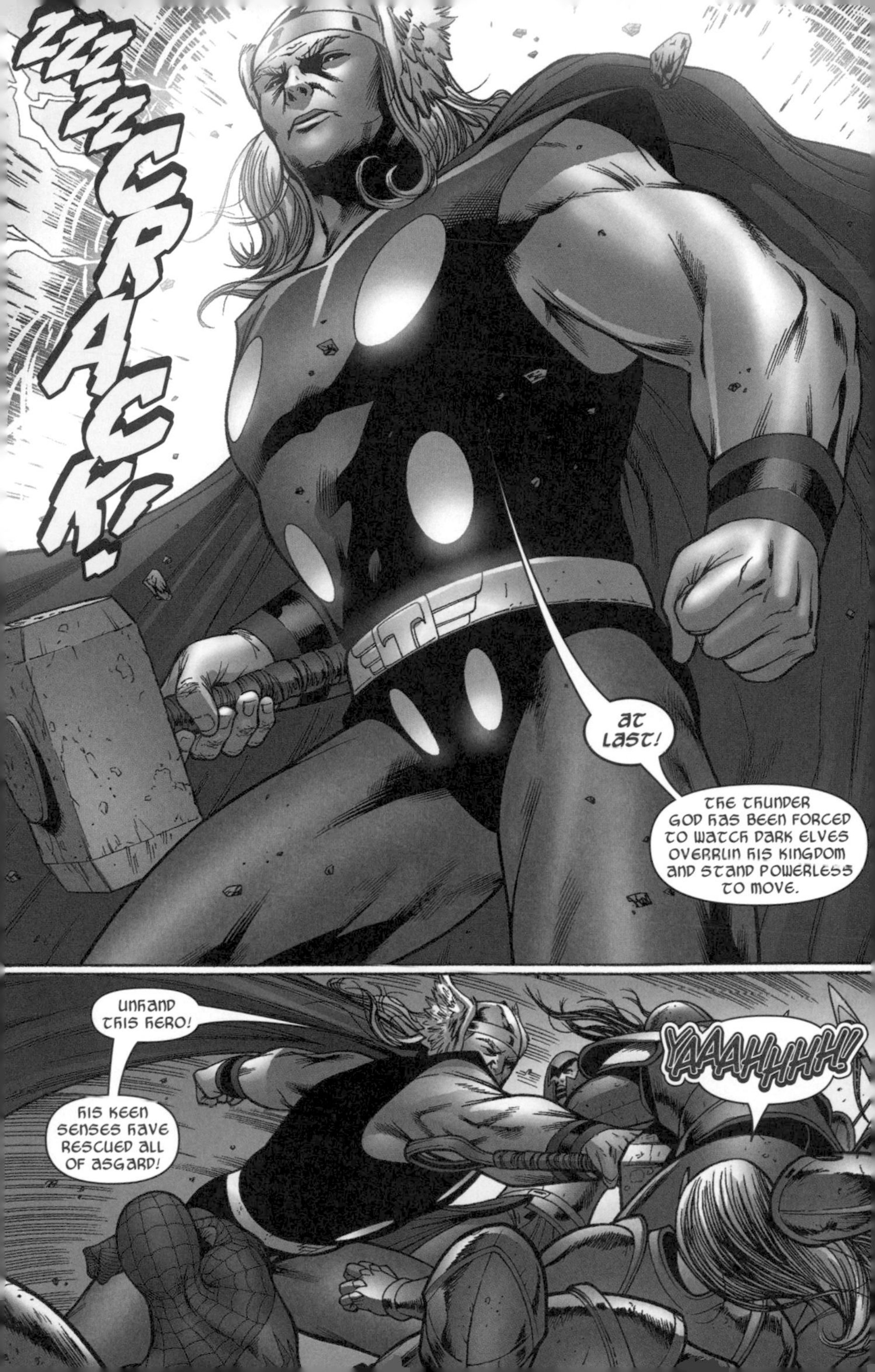
ZZZZZZCRACK!
AT LAST!
THE THUNDER GOD HAS BEEN FORCED TO WATCH DARK ELVES OVERRUN HIS KINGDOM AND STAND POWERLESS TO MOVE.
UNHAND THIS HERO!
HIS KEEN SENSES HAVE RESCUED ALL OF ASGARD!
YAAAHHHH!

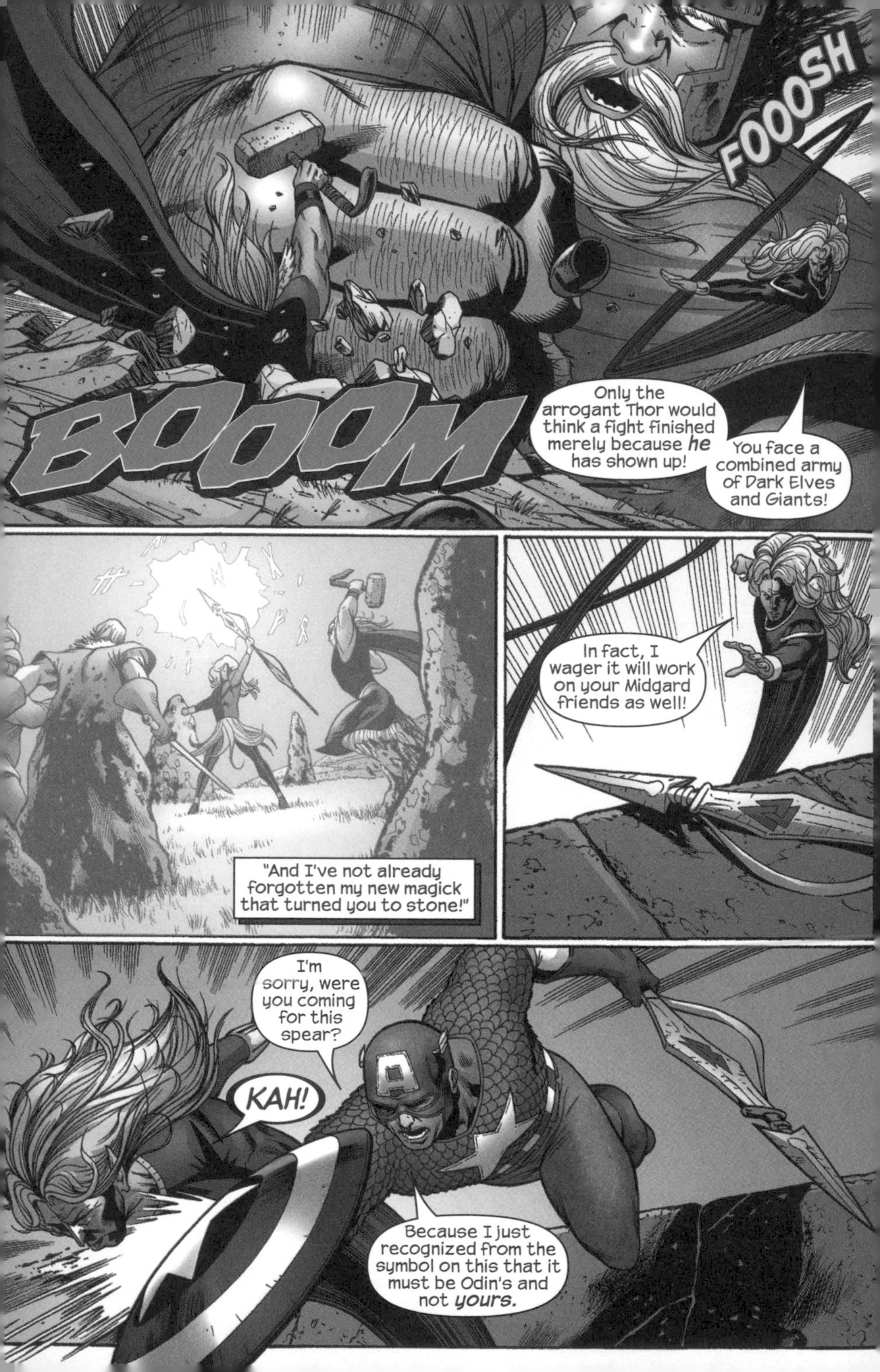
FOOOSH
BOOOM
Only the arrogant Thor would think a fight finished merely because *he* has shown up!
You face a combined army of Dark Elves and Giants!
"And I've not already forgotten my new magick that turned you to stone!"
In fact, I wager it will work on your Midgard friends as well!
I'm sorry, were you coming for this spear?
KAH!
Because I just recognized from the symbol on this that it must be Odin's and not *yours.*

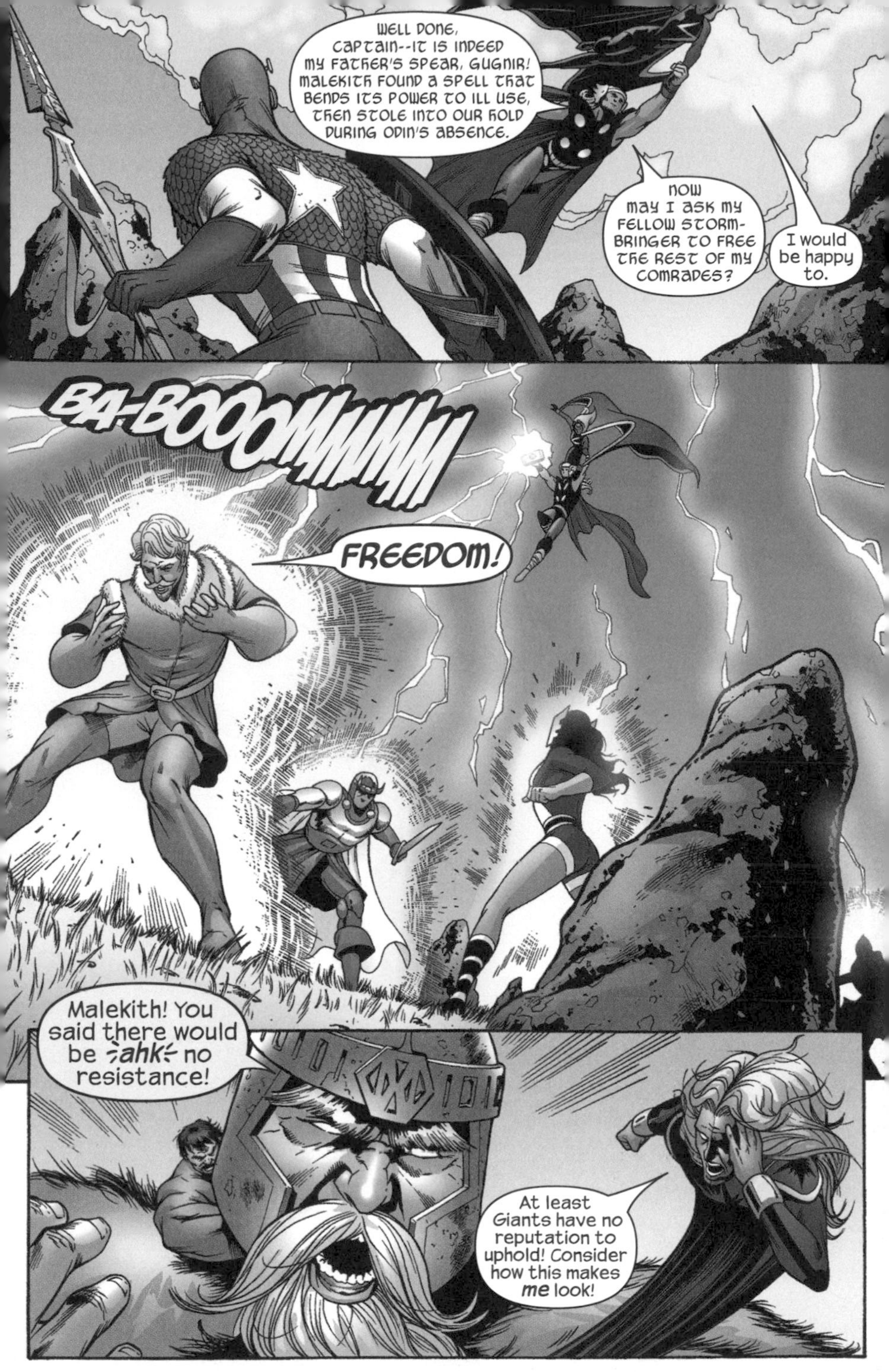
WELL DONE, CAPTAIN--IT IS INDEED MY FATHER'S SPEAR, GUGNIR! MALEKITH FOUND A SPELL THAT BENDS ITS POWER TO ILL USE, THEN STOLE INTO OUR HOLD DURING ODIN'S ABSENCE.
NOW MAY I ASK MY FELLOW STORM-BRINGER TO FREE THE REST OF MY COMRADES?
I would be happy to.
BA-BOOOMMMMM
FREEDOM!
Malekith! You said there would be -ahk- no resistance!
At least Giants have no reputation to uphold! Consider how this makes *me* look!

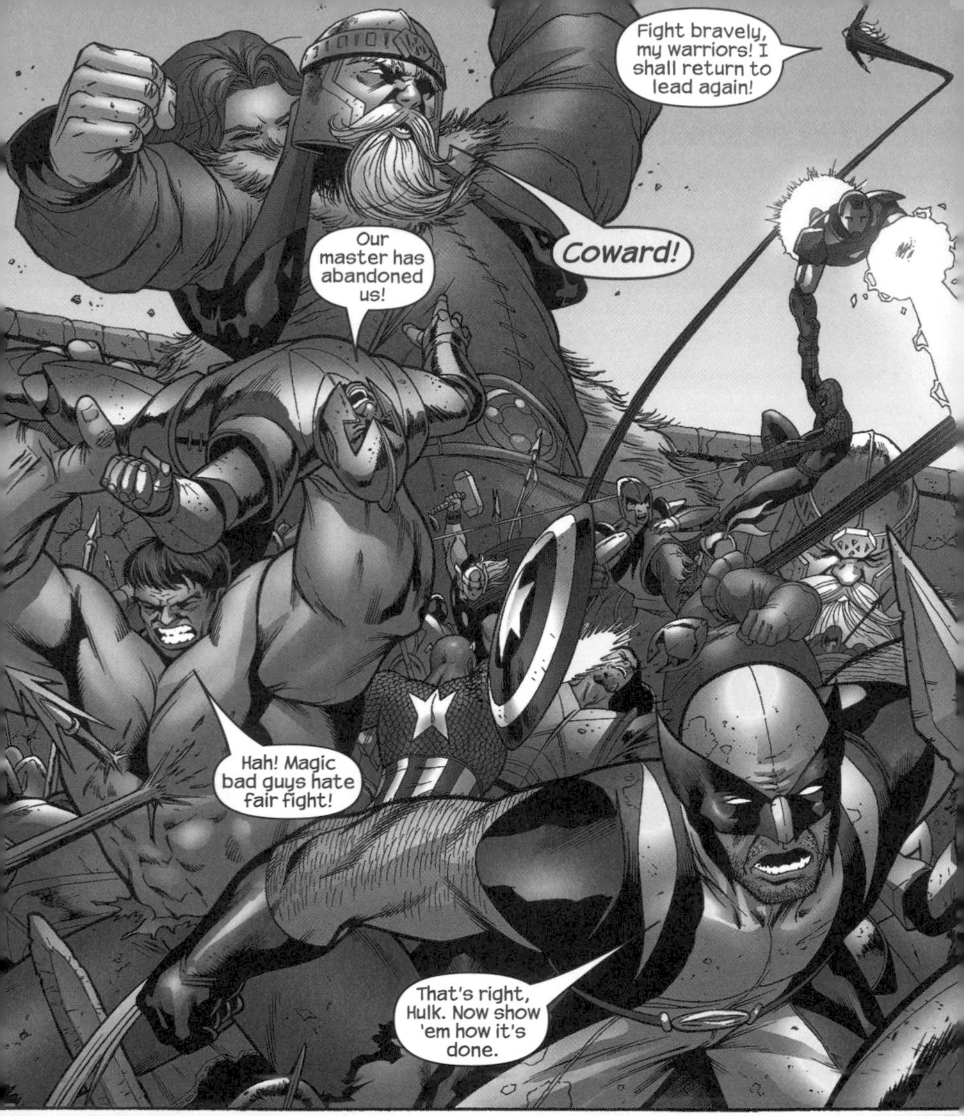
Fight bravely, my warriors! I shall return to lead again!
Coward!
Our master has abandoned us!
Hah! Magic bad guys hate fair fight!
That's right, Hulk. Now show 'em how it's done.

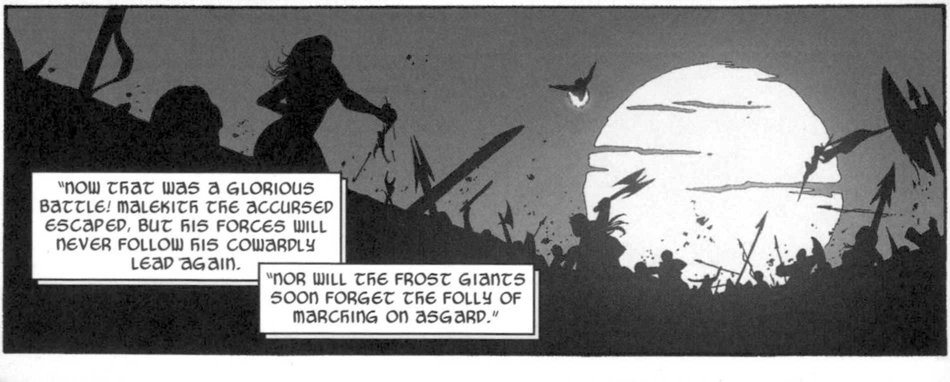
"NOW THAT WAS A GLORIOUS BATTLE! MALEKITH THE ACCURSED ESCAPED, BUT HIS FORCES WILL NEVER FOLLOW HIS COWARDLY LEAD AGAIN.
"NOR WILL THE FROST GIANTS SOON FORGET THE FOLLY OF MARCHING ON ASGARD."